The Journey to Overcoming Writer's Block

―――― ✅✅ ――――

Master Routines to Boost Your Creative Mind and Cure Procrastination Forever

Roger Willis

Your Free Gift

As a way of saying thank you for your purchase, I wanted to offer you a free bonus eBook called **5 Incredible Hypnotic Words to Influence Anyone.**

Download the free guide here:
https://www.subscribepage.com/b1b5i8

If you're trying to persuade or influence other people, then words are the essential tool you have to master.

As humans, we interact with words, and we shape the way we think through words, we express ourselves through words. Words evoke feelings and can talk to the reader's subconscious.

In this free guide, you'll **discover 5** insanely useful words that you can easily use to start hypnotizing anyone in conversation.

CONTENTS

INTRODUCTION

> *"People on the outside think there's something magical about writing, that you go up in the attic at midnight and cast the bones and come down in the morning with a story, but it isn't like that. You sit in back of the typewriter and you work, and that's all there is to it."*
> *- Harlan Ellison*

You've been there, haven't you?

Staring at a blank notebook or empty document on your computer waiting for something to happen but nothing does. Four hours later, you're still in the same spot feeling drained and 250 words to show for it. What should you do? Succumb to the misery of feeling stuck and locked out of inspiration?

Creatives from all walks of life have experienced this block, not just writers. Inspiration can become so elusive as any creative person will tell you. Playwright, Paul Rudnick said:

> *"Writing is 90 percent procrastination: reading magazines, eating cereal out of the box, watching infomercials. It's a matter of doing everything you can to avoid writing, until it is about four in the morning and you reach the point where you have to write."*

Staying up until four in the morning may not be the case for every writer, but the man has a point. There's a lot of behind the scenes stuff that most writers don't divulge. For a novice just starting to work on their first or second book, things can get pretty scary when the process isn't as perfect as they'd pictured in their head. That's what this book is going to help you with — the imperfections and struggles of writing.

If you're one of those people who assume that a secret muse sits on the shoulders of great writers making sure they always have inspiration, then you're seriously naive.

Writing is hard work, takes discipline, and requires perseverance, consistency, and the right tools to turn into something substantial.

I dare you to find any good or great writer who does not testify to experiencing writer's block at some stage in their writing career. Even a prolific writer like Virginia Woolf struggled with feelings of inadequacy during her career. She said:

"Anyone moderately familiar with the rigors of composition will not need to be told the story in detail; how he wrote and it seemed good; read and it seemed vile; corrected and tore up; cut out; put in; was in ecstasy; in despair; had his good nights and bad mornings; snatched at ideas and lost them; saw his book plain before him and it vanished; acted people's parts as he ate; mouthed them as he walked; now cried; now laughed; vacillated between this style and that; now preferred the heroic and pompous; next the plain and simple; now the vales of Tempe; then the fields of Kent or Cornwall, and could not decide whether he was the most divine genius or the greatest fool in the world."

Indeed, every creative person has experienced that feeling of being dragged in the mud. It may not be a frequent occurrence, but I can assure you, it happens even to the best of us.

The main issue I have when I look around at books that inform on writer's block is that most people position the writer's block as the villain of your writing career. It is considered to be something horrible and negative. But what if that's not entirely accurate? What if the real culprit is your ignorance? Ouch! That's a tough one to swallow.

And if you are the type of writer looking for a book that will help validate and pin the blame on things that are beyond your control, then this isn't the book for you.

This book is for writers who genuinely want to increase their understanding of what writer's block is and how to best overcome it whenever it does show up. It is explicitly going to help you if you're the type of person that prefers to take ownership of your life and actions, rather than seek out excuses. And if that's you, then stick around, because I am about to give you some nuggets that will undoubtedly transform your perception of writer's block.

CHAPTER 1

What is Writer's Block?

"I suppose I do get 'blocked' sometimes but I don't like to call it that. That seems to give it more power than I want it to have. What I try to do is write. I may write for two weeks 'the cat sat on the mat, that is that, not a rat,' you know. And it might be just the most boring and awful stuff. But I try. When I'm writing, I write. And then it's as if the muse is convinced that I'm serious and says, 'Okay. Okay. I'll come.'"
- Maya Angelou

A two-time best-selling author recently shared with me that he has been stuck for four months on the story he's developing. He wrote a chapter, then felt the pull away from that piece to another. It was troubling for him because the first two books he's authored happened rather smoothly. And given the fact that he's a man who likes to keep his commitments and get work done, the delay with this upcoming book is starting to keep him up at night.

Raise your hand if you've been in a similar situation. My hand is definitely up! I could come up with numerous reasons why this author might be going through this "block" and will name most of them in just a bit, but before getting to that, I want to make you aware of the same truth I shared with him.

Writer's block is that state in which an author feels unable to proceed with his or her writing; when one cannot think of what to write next. Unfortunately, most people have turned it into some kind of a medical condition (which it isn't by the way), like a virus that takes control of the creative process and renders you inefficient. What's even crazier is that writers think that their case is special and unique, which, again - isn't.

Let me ask you this: Have you ever met a person working in a less creative career who complained about experiencing "blocks" the way we writers love to do? If you're honest, the answer is no. A cubicle dweller will complain about Monday Blues or the 3 p.m. slump but never about a creative block. In no other industry have I encountered professionals speaking about being prevented from doing their work by some unforeseen, all-powerful force that is beyond their control - except with creatives.

I'm not trying to be mean here, but I want to give it to you straight, so you can finally stop falling into the trap so many of us land in.

I think the reason we never hear about a "doctor's block" or an "engineer's block" is because few professions require the honesty and self-reflection that writing does. I mean, as a writer, we are continually mining our life experiences, and spinning that information into beautiful prose for the world to consume and enjoy. It is no joke, my friend, and from that vantage point, it's easy to see why writer's block does exist.

The block is your pre-emptive defense against judgment. It's an internal conflict, an invisible wall between yourself and the public, and usually the safety net answer that you give when you don't want to divulge any more information about the book you haven't written.

When you tell people you have writer's block, they offer empathy, compassion, and understanding. Best of all, they leave you alone without questioning the integrity of your work or your capabilities as a writer because of the blame for underperformance shifts to this invisible villain - writer's block.

So, if you genuinely want to overcome writer's block, you also need to get more real with yourself. Writer's block only exists in your head. It is not a medical condition or an external force more significant than you. It is something internal that can only be handled from within your creative mind.

What Causes Writer's Block?

Now that you've heard the harsh truth about what writer's block is, here's the real problem that's messing with your creative output.

- Fear
- Doubt
- Poor research
- Distractions
- Fatigue
- Imposter syndrome
- Lack of structure and organization
- Laziness
- Busyness
- Perfectionism

After writing daily for the last decade or so, I can assure you, fear and self-doubt remain the highest suspects whenever I hit a snag. I know every writer is different, so maybe your reality and the root cause behind your writer's block might be different. Still, in my fact, the biggest hindrance I encounter in my writing career, as well as those of fellow authors, boils down to fear.

Discovering what the root cause of your block is doesn't fix the problem. That's called gaining self-awareness, which is an essential first step. Once you do have awareness, action toward a resolution must take place. Writer's block will not magically fix itself. If you want to make writing a career and you want to get paid for what you write, it must become a habit.

So, here's a simple three-step process to help you go within and figure out what's holding you back.

STEP ONE:

Become aware and acknowledge the resistance

I want you to become aware of and recognize this growing within you that makes it hard to sit and write. Rather than seeing this block as something negative, I challenge you to see it as a tool that you can use to your advantage.

If you are experiencing resistance, it means there's a disconnect, and your creative juices will be restricted for whatever reason. It is your opportunity to level up as a writer and break new ground.

In life, we are either growing or dying. There is no such thing as neutral ground. And so even with your writing project, each new book is an experience that will cause you to grow and level up, especially when you do it right. You will never be the same person you were before starting this book.

So, when you realize consciously and subconsciously that your current "comfort zone" is being challenged, you should get all the more encouraged because the only time an internal conflict occurs, and our minds start to self-sabotage, is when something new and vital is well underway.

STEP TWO:

Name it to tame it

Now that you acknowledge there's nothing wrong with you and that your inner conflict is part of your growth, ask yourself what is going on? Why do you feel stuck or disconnected from your creative flow? It is the step where you identify the root problem - not the symptom.

Is it fear of failure? Is it fear of being rejected? Are you still battling with the feeling that you're not good enough? Do you feel like you're not talented enough, worthy enough, resilient enough? Or are you simply exhausted? What is it that underlies the symptoms you're experiencing?

For most of us, fear is the underlying root problem that causes a disconnect, and we end up feeling stuck.

One of my author friends worked for eighteen months to produce an epic romance novel, which ended up being a New York Times bestseller.

A few months after that success, he decided to work on a new book project. A few weeks into it, excitement turned into anxiety and worry because he felt the pressure of producing something as epic as the first book.

He was already stressing about getting the book published in time; he struggled with lots of insecurities, wondering if his best work was already behind him. He got scared about what his new raving audience would think of him if they saw how hard it was to complete the second chapter and worse yet, what if they thought it was a complete horse poop?

All these strangling thoughts while working on the book led to a severe block of his creativity. It was as though the characters from his book had taken a vacation, and he couldn't find them anywhere.

He tried walking, summoning them through meditation, drinking water, and lemon, but nothing happened. They had vanished! To the rest of the world, however, he was playing it cool, pretending that he didn't have "enough time" to work on the new book.

I only got to hear about the self-manufactured torture chamber he was living on one Friday night when he had a bit too much to drink and cracked under the influence. Until he was willing to release that tension, acknowledge that something was wrong, and indeed identify the underlying fears that block would hijack and hinder his progress.

STEP THREE:

Face your worst fears

The next step for you is to summon your courage, get your game face on, and play out your worst-case scenario. In other words, go face to face with that lion that's on your path. Usually, when I do this, I discover the lion was a stuffed teddy. So, at this point, having determined what's wrong, ask yourself - what's the worst that could happen if I did fail? Would that destroy my entire career? Would I die? Most of the time, our worst fears only seem life-threatening and paralyzing because they are hiding behind the shadows of mental darkness. Bring those thoughts and fears out into the light, scrutinize them objectively, and you realize that fear doesn't hold much water.

I used to struggle with the fear of failure. Writing something that no one appreciates or enjoys. And so, I decided whenever that thought or emotion came up during my writing, I would schedule a face-to-face meeting and play out the worst-case scenario. Could I fail with this book? Sure. Would that destroy my entire career in one stroke? Not likely. I would need lots of failures before I would be entirely out of the game. Of course, it is possible to keep failing until my career flops, but it's certainly not likely. Think of Michael Jordan. He is one of the greatest basketball players in history. Yet even he's a pro at failure. In the Nike commercial that Jordan did, he explained that he missed more than 9000 shots in his career. He has lost almost 300 games; failed 26 times when he was trusted to take the game-winning shot, and yet, he is still one of the greatest players. How about instead of getting tormented by what could go wrong, we focus on how amazing it will be when things go right.

> *"The best way is to always stop when you are going good and when you know what will happen next. If you do that every day, you will never be stuck. Always stop while you are going good and don't think about it or worry about it until you start to write the next day. That way your subconscious will work on it all the time. But if you think about it consciously or worry about it, you will kill it and your brain will be tired before you start."*
> *- Ernest Hemingway*

Chapter 2

Where Does Inspiration Come From?

"Creativity is an energy. It's a precious energy, and its something to be protected. A lot of people take for granted that they're a creative person, but I know from experience, feeling it in myself, it is a magic; it is an energy. And it can't be taken for granted."
- Ava DuVernay

Inspiration is a tough one to grasp logically, unlike motivation. If you look all around the Internet, what you would find is a lot of motivation. Coaches, speakers, and so-called gurus are all great at motivating the masses with videos, quotes, etc. Goal Cast is a brand that is made entirely of motivational content extracted from interviews and speeches of famous people, and they have amassed an enormous following. People love to be motivated, and many have become addicted to receiving it daily, like a drug or an espresso shot to boost adrenaline. Inspiration, on the other hand, is a different story. And it's the very thing every true writer needs to do in his or her best work. But where does it come from? Is it finite? Can you run out of it?

There was a time in my life where I believed the commonly preached B.S. that inspiration depends on one's talent. That it's finite, like a vein of quartz within a lump of rock and once mined it dries up.

The truth is, we all have unlimited potential, and there is no end to what you can do or become regardless of age, experience, or skills. Inspiration springs up from within you in continuous flow unless you create barricades or clog out those pipes that connect you to the boundless storehouse of life itself. My conviction today is that you can relate to inspiration. It's a stream, which you can discover, and as a channel for this inspiration, you can allow your work, ideas, and creativity to flow through you to show incredible results.

Inspiration comes from within you and gets activated and nurtured by your state of mind; all the things you absorb in your environment, and re-assimilate can turn into something unique and beautiful. That's why many writers speak of spending time visiting art galleries, museums, or being in nature doing activities that are entirely unrelated to writing. It's about finding experiences that make you feel more like you (the best version of yourself) and tapping more into that so that once you step back into your work, you can bring forth the message you genuinely wish to share with the world.

Mark-Anthony Turnage, a composer, once said, "forget the idea that inspiration will come to you like a flash of lightning. It's much more about hard graft."

It's easy to feel inspired to write when you're in the zone; when your muse is right there in front of you, and all conditions are just right. But I want to focus on those times when you have to write, but nothing comes to mind. Thinking about the fact that you feel stuck only elevates the problem, and since frustration is painful, you procrastinate even more. Time ticks by; you feel the deadline creep closer, and the inspiration continues to slip away as your anxiety grows. What can you do during those times?

Stop forcing yourself to feel inspired, stop being passive about it, and stop waiting for it to fall on your lap while lying on your couch because it won't. I know you've heard from many artists this notion that inspiration can just strike out of nowhere. One moment you're in complete darkness; the next, you're off to the races. The Greeks came up with the concept of a "Muse" for this very reason. But waiting on a flash of creative energy seemingly from the gods of creativity isn't always the best idea, especially if you're serious about overcoming a block.

There are simple things you can do that can help stir up your inspiration and connect you back to that high-flying streak of creativity. After starting famous writers and other artists, I have compiled together a few hacks of my own to help produce my flow of inspiration whether or not my Muse is playing hard to get.

Nurture and nourish yourself with activities and experiences that fill you up as a person.

You must remember that you cannot pour water from an empty vessel. Half the battle of overcoming your block is about figuring out how to refill and refuel yourself.

Learn something completely new.

For me, this helps stir up my creativity and inspiration, especially when I learn something that's totally off my comfort zone.

It could be an online course on marketing, coding, or drawing. These seemingly unrelated activities to your current project (as long as you enjoy it) could all help inspire some new type of creativity. Sometimes, you don't even have to finish the course.

Learn to mute out that voice that speaks negatively about your work.

It is something we must all learn to do because learning to silence that voice of internal judgment has a direct impact on our creativity and inspiration.

There's nothing wrong with being critical of your work, maybe even comparing your past work with the present or with peers that you admire, but when it comes to actual writing, you need to be all invested. You must believe that you've got what it takes.

Ask yourself questions you can't answer.

I find that going above and beyond ordinary human awareness and logic helps me reconnect with that frequency of creativity that I like.

Who am I? Why am I here? What is the meaning of life? Does any of this really matter? What is eternity? These are all questions that none of us have definite answers to but could help stir up something within you that jumpstarts your creative flow.

Knowing that you have access to an endless stream of inspiration and creativity is one thing. Being able to keep that connection unimpeded is another. Often even when we do make this realization, we still get caught up in belief systems that create blocks. Your beliefs play a significant role in the creation of your conditions, so find a way to work on getting the right perspective. Creativity and inspiration are yours anytime you need it as long as you don't let the causes described in chapter two get in the way.

"If you get stuck, get away from your desk. Take a walk, take a bath, go to sleep, make a pie, draw, listen to music, meditate, exercise; whatever you do, don't just stick there scowling at the problem. But don't make telephone calls or go to a party; if you do, other people's words will pour in where your lost words should be. Open a gap for them, create a space. Be patient."
- Hilary Mantel

CHAPTER 3

What's Holding You Back?

If you've read each word and made it this far, there are a few assumptions I can make about you. You want to become a great writer with stunning works of art that readers can't stop talking about. Maybe this has been a dream of yours since childhood, and you want to produce books that touch hearts and change lives. It could be a full-time career or something part-time but one thing for sure, you've read every piece of advice you could find. Write every day! Sit on the keyboard and bleed. Create daily rituals, and don't skip them at all costs. Forget all that! I mean, if it were working, you wouldn't be reading a book on overcoming writer's block. You need a different approach because something's still holding you back from unleashing your full potential.

What I want to do (with your permission) is to redirect your efforts into something more unconventional. As I said before, your writer's block exists within you. So, the thing that's holding you back isn't going to be solved by any external force. More often than not, what holds you back comes from a developed habit, not a one-time thing. We are creatures of habit, and these habits either support us as we move toward our goals or hinder us from undermining our ability to achieve. I won't sugarcoat this. Becoming a great writer is going to be difficult, especially if you're living with a slew of habits that aren't supportive of your goals. Do a self-check now to see if any of these pokes something within you.

You get sidetracked easily

For example, it's time to write, but before you start, this urge to answer just one quick email or quickly scroll through Facebook suddenly takes over. Pretty soon, your allocated writing time is over, and you've barely written a page of your book. So, you promise yourself you'll do better next time, but we all know what that develops into overtime.

You feel the need to be perfect

Continually striving for perfection sets you up for failure as a writer. Stephen King, a prolific writer who has sold hundreds of millions of books, many of which are made into movies and comics, shares solid advice, *"Write with the door closed, rewrite with the door open."* Writing is intimate, and you should feel free enough to be raw and real with your words, especially at first. Have you been setting unattainable standards for yourself?

Old wounds and past failures weigh you down.

Just because something didn't work out in the past doesn't mean it won't work out now. Failure is part of becoming successful. I have learned to wear my failures and rejections like badges of honor, and you be should too. No one ever succeeds without experiencing some kind of failure.

"Carrie" by Stephen King was rejected 30 times before finally being accepted by a publisher. "Harry Potter and the Sorcerer's Stone" was rejected 12 times, and J.K. Rowling was told, *"not to quit her day job!"* This list is endless, not just with writers but even artists. For example, Jay-Z had to start his record label to publish his music because no one else believed in him (and he's now a billionaire by the way). All this to say, failure and rejection should not be the poison that destroys your potential for greatness.

You're always looking for approval

Seeking and waiting for approval or validation can also hold you back and create a block in your creativity. If you get too caught up in what others think of you (including your audience), then you'll stop actively listening within where real insights and inspiration come from. Training to gain the approval of others is futile and could easily hold you back. It isn't to say you shouldn't take in feedback and opinion from others. There is a time and a place for that. You are your own person, living with your reservoir of insights, and a message of truth that you are to channel through this book. To make it work, you really must learn to stand on your own two feet. There is no other way to become a great writer.

You have self-doubt

It is by far the biggest issue I feel most writers face. It is a dream killer and the poison that disconnects you from your creativity and inspiration. Self-doubt is such a big issue I am discussing it more in-depth in the next chapter. The critical thing to realize here is that as long as self-doubt dials up, every attempt to produce something incredible will be stymied up.

You underestimate the importance of discipline and persistence

A lot of writers start hot and motivated then quickly fizzle out because they fall for the flawed assumption that talent and lots of caffeine are all you need to write a book. Sure, skill helps, and if you are that type of writer who needs caffeine, you'll want to stock up. But what it comes down to is discipline and persistence. That is what gets you to the finish line. You've got to figure out a way to stick to your project, work tirelessly and enthusiastically until you see it through. I'm sharing more about this in the last chapter of this book.

CHAPTER 4

How to Deal with

Self-Doubt

A study was conducted not too long ago about genius. The exploration was around trying to understand what happens in a person's life that is living what might be called a genius life. The research began with the premise that "genius" is the number of modalities with which one takes in information and can synthesize or make use of that information. What the researchers discovered was that the number of patterns (you know you could receive information in with your five senses and also intuitively, imaginatively, intellectually, and perceptively) were all common to every one of us. We all possess the ability to take in information through all these different mediums. However, when all are working together in harmony, like an entire orchestra, there is what we call genius.

So, they were exploring what happens in people's lives who live this genius life, and they discovered that almost ninety-nine percent of all babies operate at a genius level for roughly the first eighteen to twenty-four months of their lives.

And if you pause to think this through for a moment, it does make sense. I mean the learning curve each one of us goes through to be able to discover how to control our hands and legs is incredible. If you watch a little infant staring at their hand or foot, it's as if it is something apart from themselves. The baby must learn how to incorporate bringing the whole body into a system, and they must shape ideas, learn words, crawl, and eventually walk. All this learning occurs in that first phase of life, and it's hyper-accelerated. In my opinion, those first few months of life have such a huge learning curve, perhaps beyond anything most of us ever achieve for the rest of our lives. Think about it: We do come into this world as geniuses.

According to the study, by the time we are five years old, only twenty percent of us are operating at a genius level. By the time we are twenty, only two percent are working at a genius level! What the heck happens to us? What mutes out those capacities that are ours?

Well, the research said that the disconnect occurs systematically and over long periods. And all of it can be attributed to this one thing: The learned voice of internal judgment.

We start to doubt. We make ourselves wrong and get into the habit of looking outside ourselves for strength, validation, approval, and opinions about what we can be, what we can do, and what's possible for us.

In other words, that research helped me realize that as we grow up, we learn to be condition-based in our thinking because that is the primary programming on planet earth. That's how most people live their entire lives. And perhaps that's fine if you spend your entire career in a cubicle, but for us as writers, it becomes a significant hindrance to our success.

The root cause of self-doubt is fear itself, and there are many variations of it, but the bottom line is you will struggle and continue to battle with failure and writer's block if you don't get a handle on that voice that generates self-doubt.

Your self-doubt is to you as kryptonite is to Superman. It's also the culprit behind imposter syndrome. It is one emotion we all struggle with, and it can ruin everything because the more we question ourselves and second guess our actions, the more our creativity gets stifled. Think of it this way: the biggest clogger creating a block in your flow of creativity and inspiration is almost always fear and self-doubt.

Jenny, an award-winning writer, shared her frustrations with me a few weeks ago:

"I'm not clinically depressed per se, but I have times when the self-doubt is so rampant, I have a hard time focusing on my work. I worry a lot. I'm anxious about

29

how I'll make a living as a writer. I love it, but so far, it's only made me enough money for a nice dinner. I'm also worried people won't like the book I'm currently working on because I'm not sure the themes are deep enough. And I keep wondering if the characters are well developed. It's crippling. And I'm so afraid to fail, which is odd considering I don't have much to fail from. I try to remind myself that things will work out, but it's easier said than done, you know?"

I think we can all agree that we've experienced similar frustrations. Self-doubt is creativity poison that creeps up on new writers as well as full-time professionals. Making money, getting famous, or becoming successful doesn't eliminate self-doubt, but the right kind of strategies can help you deal with it for good. Here are a few good ones to test out.

Strategies for Handling Self-Doubt:

Look at the story itself

Just take a moment and ask yourself the following questions:

Why am I finding it difficult to trust my thoughts?
Why is the book failing to develop the way I want
it to?
Is it because I'm trying to fix it into the wrong
shape?
Have I lost sight of my Why?
Or is it something else?

Understand that having that negativity surging up
within isn't by accident. Self-doubt and fear take
up residence in your mental space for a good
reason, and as long as you take the time to assess
why you feel the way you do or why things are
going badly, you can quickly evict them and get
back to work.

Say stop

As soon as you become aware of the inner conflict
rising, don't let things spin out of control. Instead,
take yourself to an environment that energizes
you and have a talk with that doubtful part of
yourself. I usually go to the beach, a river, a lake,
a pond, or any other body of water I can easily find
and have a heart to heart with myself.

You could present the current situation to
yourself and say something like, "No! I say no. We
are not going down that road again." By doing
this, you are disrupting that thought pattern and
showing yourself who's boss in your mind.

Order a giant dose of optimism

Is there someone in your life who is always overflowing with enthusiasm, optimism, motivation, and that bubbly energy that makes everything more radiant? Call them up and arrange an in-person meeting. Spend some time with that person and let that optimism flow over to you.

Find your source of optimism

In the unlikely event that there is no one in your life to fill that order, consider finding a podcast, audiobook, YouTube channel, or a book that can help you shift your self-doubt into optimism. Any piece of material that can help you think constructively of this challenge should do the trick.

Some people swear by Tony Robbins and his loud, aggressive nature. For some, it's spiritual teachers or motivational speakers like Les Brown. Whatever works for you, just do it for a few sessions and let the doubts melt away.

Make a list of all your achievements

Bring to mind all the successful experiences you've had, even if they have nothing to do with writing. Recalling those moments of fulfillment and satisfaction is a great way to shift from fear and self-doubt because you show yourself how amazing you've been in the past.

Scientists tell us that our brains are conditioned to actively recall a negative experience, even though it's not healthy for us for survival reasons. I think when we were still living in caves next to wild animals, that was a good thing, but in today's world, you don't need a constant reminder of the mishaps.

What you need is a reminder of all the good you've been able to produce. Be real about this, and don't try to force yourself into something you don't believe.

If you revisit your past experiences and see how well things have gone many times despite those self-doubts, then it becomes easier to let go and refocus your energy and take positive actions going forward.

Stop beating yourself up about having self-doubt!

Doing this makes things only worse and more difficult, have you noticed? It becomes a vicious cycle and feels like you can't get out of a recurring time loop. Beating yourself up because you're not moving forward only keeps you stuck in the very state you're trying to escape.

What I like to do in these moments is to parent myself and soothe myself, as a mother would her young child. I show myself compassion and use kind, loving words with a very empathic tone whenever I speak to myself. Then instead of trying to solve the whole problem or get clarity over the entire book, I simply ask myself what's one tiny baby step I could take that day to feel like I had accomplished something. I find that shifting my focus to taking baby steps is a great way to rebuild my momentum with no pressure or grand expectations.

Use the magic statement

"You might be right, but..."
I use this statement all the time whenever that negative inner chatter comes up. For example, when the thought comes up, "people won't like this new book."

I immediately counter that thought with, " You might be right, but I won't know until I finish writing it and give them a chance to read it."

Or I might hear, "You're not a writer; people will discover that you're not that good soon."

My response to that is, " You might be right, but until that day comes, I will just keep playing this role because it feels nice thinking of myself as a writer."

See how easy it can be to catch those shots of poison and dissolve them? The earlier you seize them, the less damage they do. So, what responses can you create now using this magic statement?

CHAPTER 5

Tips on How to Manage Your Energy

Just as professional athletes prepare and train before participating in a competition, you should also get into the habit of prepping and training your mind to write before starting a new project. Writing takes up a lot of energy. Even though it may not seem like it, writing is every bit as demanding as physical labor, which means you're expending a lot of energy. Unless you find a way to keep generating that energy, it doesn't matter how much time you've got to complete a book. Each time you sit in front of your blank page, if your brain isn't cooperating, nothing good will happen. To help you avoid or at least get out of that uncomfortable situation, let's discuss good practices for writing:

1. You need to have a unique system. I call this the secret sauce for finishing your book. We delve into this in the last chapter of this book.

2. You must start taking care of your physical health. Unhealthy writers won't do as well or enjoy the process of writing (which is equally as crucial as finishing). Your mind and body are connected in ways that even science cannot fully comprehend. When the physical body is not thriving, the brain cannot thrive or perform well. The type or length of physical activity that you do doesn't matter; you just need to be fully immersed in it. And with physical activity comes watching how you fuel your body. I know it can be hard for you to stop working on a project to make a healthy meal. Grabbing a coffee and eating cereals for dinner is the more comfortable option, but if you want to succeed long-term as a writer and in life, invest in healthier eating habits.

3. You must train your brain. Have you read the book "Super Brain" by Dr. Deepak Chopra and Dr. Rudolph E. Tanzi? It's an epic revelation of how wrong we are about the brain and its potential. In the book, Dr. Chopra says, "One of the unique things about the human brain is that it can only do what it thinks it can do. The minute you say, "my memory isn't what it used to be..." you are training your brain to live up to your diminished expectations. Low expectations mean low results. The first rule of the super brain is that your brain is always eavesdropping on your thoughts. As it listens,

it learns. If you teach it about limitation, your brain will become limited."

Now imagine what you are training your brain into whenever you say, "I have writer's block." One of the best ways to start preparing your brain is to develop consistency with your schedule so that you can write at the same time each day. You should also check out the long list of strategies I've shared in the next chapter, as some of them are specifically designed to help with this.

4. You must intentionally design and maximize your focus and relaxation times. Yes, you read it right. It's not just about prioritizing your productivity and focus. You need relaxation just as much, so you need to find activities or experiences that help create that balance between output and input of your creativity and inspiration. Your mind and brain need time to reset. For some people, relaxation means doing absolutely nothing! That's not resting for me; it's torture!

Besides sleeping, I give my brain time to reset by doing things I consider fun like walking, shopping, listening to Opera, watching stand-up comedy, and sometimes playing chess. I have a friend who resets by spending some time in church a few days a week volunteering as well as going to the art museum. We are all unique as individuals, so find experiences that help inspire and invigorate you, then schedule them into your calendar.

5. Work on your discipline. Without discipline, you won't get very far. Most people don't realize that talent alone isn't enough to make anyone successful regardless of their chosen field. I love writing with all my heart; if I stopped writing, my whole world would crumble - and yet, even I have to apply a lot of discipline to perform at the level that I do. Discipline and perseverance are not negatives in the world of writing; they are pre-requisites as much as passion is. Let's talk more about how you can amp up your discipline.

Good Practices for Increasing Self-Discipline

- Start writing every day
- Get an accountability partner
- Consider starting a blog for your book
- Read every day
- Change your perception of willpower
- Set smaller S.M.A.R.T goals within your writing project
- Create a reward system for yourself
- Learn to embrace discomfort
- Cultivate physical, mental, and emotional self-care rituals

- Create habits that support your writing
- Leverage technology
- Shift your perception of hard work
- Redefine what success means to you
- Work on gaining control over your emotions
- Identify your weaknesses and build support structures around them
- Track and measure your progress

Increasing Your Productivity

If you take care of your mind, your mind will take care of you. It's as simple as that. There is no conspiracy trying to take down your writing empire unless you help fuel it from within.

There's no shortcut to maintaining focus and productivity. It will not come by default, especially as you get older. An exhausted, unhealthy, stressed out, and a negative mindset can only produce writings that are subpar at best. The more you feed and nurture your mind with the right stuff, the better it will serve you.

That means you need to be deliberate and intentional with your activities so that everything you do optimizes for success. If you want to write well, stay focused, inflow, and highly productive, you'll need to make some changes.

Last year I invested quite a significant amount of time researching productivity and came across Edward Deci, a researcher who wrote a book titled

'Why We Do What We Do.' In the book, Deci explains that when someone has six positive interactions with one negative, they are 31% more productive. During his research, Deci noticed a trend in positive interactions vs. negative and how they each influence productivity. Fascinating stuff.

Simple as it seemed to me at the time, I decided to put this theory to the test. I started writing out on my journal each morning before getting into my writing - why I was grateful to be working on this particular book. At first, it was simple things like I'm thankful for my ability to write clearly and effectively communicate my message with the world. A few days in, even those simple sentences started disappearing because I felt like I had already named everything I appreciate about my work. But I refused to let myself off the hook, and one year later, I am still doing this exercise every day. I bring gratitude to each project I want to work on, and I shifted my perspective from "I have to do it" to " I want to do it."

Ready to become a brilliant writer? Here's what you need to do:

Establish habits that help you perform at an optimum level

For example, don't stay up till 3 am to write just because you've heard writers say it works. Maybe you are more of a morning person; staying up late would only lead to - you guessed it - writer's block.

Get to know your body clock

Following up on that first tip, you need to self-investigate and identify your most productive hours. We all have natural rhythms that influence our ability to focus and produce. The secret here is to match your writing time to your most productive hours of the day. Do you know your body clock?

Take regular mental breaks

Even a short break, when done strategically, can give you that burst of inspiration and creativity needed to get you to the next chapter. The moment you feel mental fatigue kicking in, step away from the screen even if it's just for a few moments. Go for a walk, stretch, or spend a few minutes outside soaking in some sun.

Declutter your workspace or desktop

I didn't just make this one up by the way, even though it resonates with me. Researchers have found that when there's too much stuff in your field of view, it has a measurable impact on productivity. They found that too much clutter causes people to lose brain power and necessary focus. I found that by cleaning up my desktop, my mind would feel calmer, open, and at ease, which somehow enables me to refocus and get back into it.

Start your gratitude journal

Your creative mind can be immensely boosted by adopting a habit of gratitude for your writing. Developing appreciation for the story you're attempting to share with the world will increase your love of writing. Keep things simple. Write what you are grateful for, and why, every day for the next 30 days, and take note of the difference it makes. Here are a few starter lines to get you going.

I am grateful for my first cup of coffee this morning because it's exactly what I need to jump into my writing fired up.

I am grateful for my computer and writing software because they make my work super easy and convenient, and my writing software keeps all online distractions away from me.

Now it's your turn.

CHAPTER 6

Strategies for Overcoming Writer's Block

Reconnect with your WHY

Simon Sinek is famous for stating - always begin with your WHY. I think this is sound advice to apply whenever you bump into that writer's block. If the words just aren't streaming through, no matter what you try, step away from that situation and take a moment in solitude.

Sit with yourself in silence and remind yourself why you are working on this project. Why is it so vital that you put this book out in the world? What is this message you want to share, and why does it matter? Get reacquainted with your reason for writing and watch that block dissolve.

Stop obsessing over that, which is beyond your control

Instead of worrying over things that you can't control, such as what the public and critics will say, whether it'll become a bestseller in record time or not, etc., focus on the next thing you're going to write. Not the entire manuscript; just that next part.

Stop writing for the world

Getting published, building a fan base, becoming famous, and making money are all great, but none of them should be the driving motive behind your writing. The point of writing is the joy of sitting down to a blank page and crafting something beautiful or funny or heart wrenching or even just meh (depending on the day). Writing is more about the journey than the destination.

All this to say, writing is a form of self-expression, not an ego boost. Get back to writing for the joy it brings you, and that sense of "stuckness" will dissipate naturally.

Give yourself time

Sometimes I think all this pressure we put on ourselves as writers chokes our creativity like weeds on a rose bush. Sometimes it's best to step back, take some time self-reflecting, reading, discovering new things, learning about being a better writer, etc. When you feel like you're facing an invisible wall, don't force things and certainly don't try to hurry things along or fuss about deadlines. There's no rush to get published, and you are allowed to take your time. Always remember that.

Stop making excuses

Yes, this is imperative because, as I said at the beginning of this book, writer's block is real only in your head. So, this idea that you can justify your procrastination and avoidance with this term, just because everyone makes it seem acceptable is total B.S. If you are experiencing that inner conflict that blocks you from your zone of genius, do something about it. Realize it's there and acknowledge that it is your responsibility to overcome this temporary setback, from this figure out the best course of action that most resonates with you.

Challenge yourself

By this, I mean, you should seek to find something constructive in this experience. It's not all bad. There are lessons to be learned, insights to be gained, and growth to be experienced that can better assist your progress as a writer. This dry gap and discomfort can be a time for you to challenge your writing skills even more. See this block as a tool and stepping stone to help elevate you to the next level. Start by listing down all the good that can come from going through this experience.

Freewrite

Set a timer and give yourself that time to freewrite. If no words come to you, then use that time jotting down loose associations and images that come to mind relative to your story. Practice what's known as stream of consciousness writing. The only rule with this tip is that your pen has to keep moving for the entire time. Not all ideas will be of value, but you might find something that can then pull you back into the actual story you want to tell.

Permit yourself to suck

That's right. I want you to allow yourself to do some bad writing. In the book "Bird by Bird" by Anne Lamott, readers are encouraged to write terrible first drafts. Lammot reassured us that we all write bad first drafts and that the lousy first draft is part of the natural progression on the path toward an excellent second draft and a great manuscript. Set aside this illusion that you need to be great right off the bat. When you were learning to walk as a child, you didn't focus on being perfect; you concentrate on making it happen. That same childlike approach should be used in your creative endeavors. By taking on that carefree approach, you'll find the pressure is gone, and I'm pretty sure even your initial work won't be half as bad as you think. Besides, if it is terrible, no one else has to see it until you're ready.

Take regular breaks

Taking breaks regularly to reset your brain, refuel and hydrate your body must be prioritized. I noticed that when I don't stop at my appointed breaks, I end up being less productive on that given day. I like to use the Pomodoro technique to make sure my breaks are planned out well.

The Pomodoro Technique

This time management technique is used widely by people across diverse industries and works like a charm for me. Invented by Francesco Cirillo in the late 1980s, it's the perfect way to break your writing into intervals, avoid fatigue, and promote productivity. Here's how to implement it. Set the mini-goal you'd like to accomplish for the day. Set the Pomodoro for twenty-five minutes and work uninterrupted on that single writing task until the timer goes off. When the Pomodoro rings, pause, take your short break. You can grab a fresh cup of coffee, soak in some sun by the window, balcony, or go outside for a few minutes, or you can do anything else that is not work-related. I like to take my mandala and color them during my short breaks while doing deep breathing exercises. After the short break, jump back into it for another session.

After four Pomodoros, take a more extended break for about 20 or 30 minutes. The way I plan out my writing time, this long break is usually for healthy eating, light exercise, or being outdoors.

There are many ways to customize and make your Pomodoro more effective, depending on your objectives and preferences. Some writers set their Pomodoro to forty-five minutes. I don't recommend anything longer because studies have shown the brain tends to tune out anyways after that duration.

Handwrite your stream of consciousness

Even if you're stuck on the current manuscript, you can still write something. We've all heard the famous statement, "a body in motion tends to remain in motion..." Make sure you write something, anything at all. It could be an entirely new story, your current feelings, an experience you just had, or whatever else comes to you. There is no right or wrong - just write.

Change locations

If you usually write in silence in the corner of the room in your basement, switch things up and spend a day in a coffee shop or a library. Sometimes the radical shift in the environment is enough to jumpstart your creative ideas.

Read a lot more than usual

You're already feeling stuck. Rather than forcing yourself to do something you're not aligned with at this moment, use this time to immerse yourself in a great book. Other people's writing can become an endless source of ideas, and who knows, something in there might get you back in the mood and inspire new thoughts.

Play

I'm being serious here. Pick a game you love that gets you all excited and immerse yourself in that for a few hours. I usually go to chess or LEGOS.

Shift your focus to someone who makes you feel good

How about interviewing a friend or just buying them coffee and spending some time with them so you can completely forget about work. Talk, laugh, listen, ask questions, and, most importantly, do something nice for them and notice the difference this makes in how you feel about yourself and life in general. Often, we like to think that work is separate from the home, but in truth, all things have a connection. The more you feel good about yourself, the more everything you do will reflect that.

Increase your physical activities

There's no better time to move your body, get a little sweat on, and improve your health than when your writing hits a snag. Perhaps your mind is trying to create some spare time for you to take care of your body. And research proves that working out improves all areas of your life, including creativity. So rather than sitting there watching Netflix or wallowing in self-pity, waiting for the writing gods to have mercy on you, go for a jog in the park or take a spin class.

Advanced strategies for overcoming writer's block

Get more structured

If you're one of those writers who scoff at the structure as something that would limit your creativity or even amplify writer's block, I'm sorry to say that's fear talking.

I am part of a writer's community where we meet up in person every three months to support, encourage, and keep each other accountable. There's a woman who joined our community about eighteen months ago, and each time she speaks, her main issue is always getting stuck halfway into her projects. During our last meet-up, I asked her what she's doing to resolve this recurring problem permanently. I brought in the concept of creating structure, and she immediately shrieked. "I'm not the type. I hate structure in my life and certainly can't write if I was forced to be more structured and organized."

Unfortunately, that mindset will keep you falling into the pit of writer's block. You need to find a way to make productivity not just probable, but inevitable.

Sleep on it

Sometimes the best medicine is to rest more. There are times when exhaustion, fatigue, or poor sleeping habits impact our ability to concentrate and focus. I found a research paper that speaks to this very truth. You can find a link to read the comprehensive research on how sleep works and the creative brain during sleep in the resource section at the end of the book. But here are some interesting insights on REM sleep and creativity.

Many people report being able to do their best work immediately after awakening. What is so special about the early morning? Research suggests the proximity to recent sleep is the key, especially given that most people have their longest stage of REM sleep just before waking in the morning. A Harvard Medical school study scientist reported that subjects could solve 30% more anagram word puzzles when tested after waking up from REM sleep than non-REM sleep. Most research published in 2012 similarly found that sleep is particularly good at helping people solve complex problems. Science has also confirmed that REM sleep allows people to become more creative. At the University of California at San Diego, researchers used a protocol called a Remote Associates Test (RAT) to quantify increases in creativity. They divided test subjects into three groups right before taking the test. One group was allowed to rest but not sleep, another was allowed to experience NREM sleep but was roused before REM, and the other was allowed to reach the REM stage. Those in the rest and NREM groups showed no increase in creativity as measured by RAT, whereas those recently woken from REM showed an increase in capacity. UC San Diego scientists also found that participants scored 40% better on a creativity test after REM sleep. REM seems to spark solutions to new creative problems better than any other stage of sleep, suggesting that "sleep on it" may be sound advice.

Need I say more?

Mind map your ideas

It is especially useful when you start feeling unclear about the direction of the story or if you're struggling with the progression of the story. A mind map is a diagram used to organize information visually. This term was coined by a British author and Television personality Tony Buzzan and can be an effective way to get you out of your writing rut. To do things right, you'll need to make sure you do the following. Revisit your original topic idea and make sure you have clarity on the desired outcome. Make sure you have a lot of creative space like a whiteboard or a table with sticky notes where you can visually create your mind map. The subject title should be the mind map title to remind you of what you are brainstorming. Add branches and topics and the sub-branches with their sub-topics without worrying about organization or flow for now. The organization comes later. Let all the ideas flow freely from your mind, and please take a break when you run out of ideas or struggle to concentrate. But always keep coming back to it after the short breaks until you feel like you've collected all of your thoughts. To make this even more practical, here are a few steps you can follow:

1. Place your main topic or chapter (depending on where you feel stuck) in the center of the whiteboard or table.

2. Close your eyes, take a deep breath, and summon the ideas to flow to you. Trust me, they will come to you, and as they do, I want you to jot them down on different sticky notes as without overthinking them. If you're using a whiteboard, draw arms and label them.

3. As more details come to you, make sub-arms from the key ideas, and write short detailed notes. If using sticky notes, try to use different colored notes for the details. It helps if you can think of all the questions your reader may ask you as they go through that particular chapter or section. Keep expanding, writing whatever comes to you in no specific order until you feel complete.

4. Now you can pick up the best ideas from your mind map and structure it or group the different areas you want to talk about depending on the flow you like.

There are lots of tools available if you want to do this digitally. I prefer a big table with lots of sticky notes, but in the resources, I am going to share a free tool that I found online that seems to do the job pretty efficiently.

Self-care practices

Although we've seen a lot more emphasis placed on self-care and mindfulness practices, I think many writers still perceive it as a luxury or "only for certain people." The truth is if you inhabit a human body, you need to practice self-care.

Why is self-care an essential part of your writing success? Because with self-care comes self-compassion, both of which are integral cornerstones to improving your relationship with yourself. I have said this before, but it bears repeating. Writer's block is all real - within you. The more you learn to heal that internal conflict that creates these blocks, the more you won't have to deal with these types of obstacles. Sounds easy, right? Well, it's not.

Learning to love yourself, trust and have faith in yourself, and feel genuine compassion for yourself when things aren't going too well, is one of the most challenging tasks you'll ever face. I still struggle with it today, and I've been working at it for years now. But I'm not talking about being self-centered or selfish. On the contrary, loving yourself deepens your ability to care for others and the work you do. Self-care isn't about procrastinating or being lazy; it's about practicing self-acceptance, becoming more mindful and aware of your thoughts, behaviors, and actions. It is also about living a balanced lifestyle, which let's be honest; most writers struggle with it.

Think of it this way: it would be impossible for an architect to construct a beautiful building on a flimsy foundation. You are no different when it comes to the construction of your masterpiece. And the foundational elements needed aren't tools or external objects. What you need is a robust internal foundation that can support all that you want to produce and share with the outer world because life is an inside-out game. Now I know, this can be a daunting idea, but I encourage you to just sleep on it and reflect on the implications that have been suggested. It is more than just self-improvement or personal development. It's about learning how to deal and relate to yourself when you feel blocked or divided inside. If you are trying to increase your inspiration and creativity, why would you call upon yourself to achieve this goal, unless a part of you already has access to boundless creativity and inspiration?

It isn't a simple question to answer, and I don't expect you to, but I do want you to start shifting perspective and get more curious. As writers, curiosity comes naturally to us. Let us use this curiousness to overcome challenges such as writer's block.

Some cool new things you can try out if you want to dive into this world of self-care and self-compassion as a strategy to overcome blocks include:

Meditation

It is one of the most natural, most accessible spiritual practices that anyone can begin. I swear by meditation and honestly believe my blocks have almost become non-recurring thanks to my commitment to meditate daily. It wasn't easy when I started. I didn't know if I was doing it right, couldn't stop thoughts from distracting me, etc. but I kept at it. Things are much better now, mainly because I stopped trying to eliminate my thoughts and started focusing on observing them instead. Experts say meditation can restructure your brain, reduce stress, give you clarity, boost immunity, and so many other amazing benefits. I'm still a novice and have much to learn, but I can already attest to the fact that something special happens when you start meditation. The demons in my head seem to be mellowing down a lot giving me enough room to focus on my craft.

Deep breathing techniques

Most of us aren't aware of the way we breathe, but in general, there are two types of breathing patterns: Thoracic, also known as chest breathing, and diaphragmatic, also known as abdominal breathing. The more anxious we become, the shallower our breathing gets, which usually means we are breathing from the chest. It causes an upset in the oxygen and carbon dioxide levels resulting in increased heart rate, muscle tension, and other physical sensations.

As you can imagine, when the blood isn't adequately circulating oxygen, the body gets stressed, which only amplifies the "blocked" state we're trying to overcome. So, a great practice to get into, especially when attempting to start writing, is to do some simple abdominal breathing exercises to connect your body, mind, and spirit. Here's something cool you can try.

Inhale slowly and deeply through your nose. Keep your shoulders relaxed. Let your abdomen expand and make sure your chest rises only a little. Then, exhale slowly through your mouth. As you blow out air, purse your lips slightly, but keep your jaw relaxed as you exhale until all the air is out. Repeat this breathing exercise for several minutes. Although you can do this exercise in any position, I recommend standing up or lying down for a more luxurious experience. Remember to focus on calming your mind or reconnecting your whole being (not thinking about how you can't think of what to write).

Yoga

Yoga can help you harmonize your body, mind, and spirit and individualized explicitly according to what your needs are at the time. There are many well-known physical benefits for doing Yoga, but there's more to it than just getting a nice workout.

Yoga will help you connect with your body and the emotions that are stored deep within. It encourages non-judgment and self-acceptance about where you are in life, and we all know this is key to overcoming blocks and moving forward. There are many types of yoga, so just do a bit of exploration and try a few classes out to see what feels right for you.

Spending time in nature

The sound of birds, the warmth of the sun, the sight of trees swaying in the wind, or waves crashing on the shore make your senses come alive and can be just what you need to rekindle your creative fire. Nature always brings healing and presents moment awareness, so take time as often as you can to be in nature, even when you're not going through writer's block.

Forgiving yourself

Often, the block sticks around longer than is necessary because you get in this vicious cycle of being angry with yourself for not writing or meeting your daily writing goal, which makes you feel worse and keeps you in the same state. When you are unable to practice self-compassion and forgiveness, a lot of energy goes to waste. That's where practicing forgiveness comes in. It's essential to stay present and accept that life is about ebb and flow. Pleasure and pain are part of your journey, and overcoming challenges is part of the mastery process. Of course, the ego prefers joy and comfort, and it's a lot easier to feel good and stay present when creativity and inspiration overflow. But the discipline gained from working through stumbling blocks as you master your craft is just as relevant and helps solidify your success. The more you understand who you are and why writing is important to you, the easier it will be to practice self-forgiveness and show yourself some compassion when you stumble.

These ideas might seem a bit too far-fetched for you, so don't test all these ideas out at once. Start small, pick one practice, and, if it feels good, keep doing it until it forms into a habit. Then select and experiment with a new one. Practicing self-care will help nurture you as a whole being and leave no areas of your life unattended. It will restore calmness and confidence in your life, which is precisely what your mind needs to start cranking out words that will keep people glued to your book.

CHAPTER 7

The Secret Sauce for Finishing Your Book

Strategies that help you manage your energy, mood, focus, and productivity are all well and good. But at the end of the day, if you want to be a great writer, you're going to need something extra. You need to master your craft. It can only come from investing a ton of time writing.

Think of Ernest Hemingway, Stephen King, Lee Child, Arthur Conan Doyle, J.K. Rowling, and so many other great writers in the past or present. The most successful writers, regardless of genre or writing style, all have one thing in common - they don't just throw words on paper whenever they feel like it. If they did, they wouldn't have become great writers.

Did you know Hemingway always wrote in the morning as soon as the sun rose? Did you know Stephen King writes 2,000 words a day, rain or shine? Here are a few more fun facts that might help you see the commitment needed to make you a great writer.

Ernest Hemingway would stick to writing about 500 words a day. Michael Crichton wrote several novels that turned into films such as Jurassic Park (which I bet you recognize). His daily word count was 10,000 words. Now that's ambitious. Kate DiCamillo is an American writer of children's fiction who set her daily goal as writing two pages a day, five days a week. It translates to about 600-900 words a day. Lee Child, a British author, is best known for his Jack Reacher novels that became films starring Tom Cruise. He has a daily goal of 1,800 words and likes to write in the afternoon, from about 12 until 6 or 7 pm.

As you can see, there is no one-size-fits-all when it comes to writing goals. There is one thing these established authors have in common; they have successfully developed a secret sauce - a writing system that works for them.

So, what is the secret sauce to finishing your book and eliminating writer's block? Develop and hone your writing system. Instead of looking for tricks and loopholes, focus on building and sticking to a productive writing system. So, let's break them into steps that are easy to follow.

STEP ONE > Collecting material

Every writer needs resources and writing material. It's your job to know what you need and where to get it before you start writing.

Here are a few places you can start mining for resources:

Research

Research on relevant forums, social media threads, and other online spaces where your ideal audience naturally hangs out to speak on the topic you're writing.

Your life history

Summon your memory and read through your old journals or photo albums for ideas.

Other people's life histories

Talk to your relatives and friends. Remember to ask high-quality questions and then listen. Your ability to listen with your head and heart will help you acquire lots of material because people love to talk about themselves.

Read books and articles

Get an audible account and subscribe to relevant podcasts. And I mean a lot of them.

Follow other writers

Observe what they are doing and try to get inspiration from them. Don't copy. Just let their ideas trigger your own.

STEP TWO > Writing

Collecting your resources and material is excellent, but none of that matters if you don't sit and write. So how do you do this? Well, aside from the obvious - literally sitting down and typing or writing by hand, there are a few other things you need to help shape this new system.

Set daily goals or daily milestones

Take the examples I shared above of different writers with their daily page or word count. You need to do the same for your writing system to work. The daily milestones help move you forward toward the achievement of the bigger goals.

Choose a start time

Some people want to write with the sunrise, and others want to write in the middle of the night. Choose a time that works for you and feels most productive then stick to it.

Create a deliberate constriction

In other words, choose to limit yourself. Bestselling novelist Jodi Picoult once said, "writer's block is having too much time on your hands. If you have a limited amount of time to write, you just sit down and do it."

STEP THREE > Honing your craft

As with any other type of mastery, if you want to become great, you must take time to work on your craft. And like any other craft, there are best practices and recognized levels of proficiency. There are so many things you can do to keep improving your art, but you must be proactive. Some people prefer to hire a writing coach or purchase a writing course to help improve their work. Others want the self-taught route, which is excellent too. So, here are a few suggestions that I've found useful.

Read a book on writing

I recommend Stephen King's book titled "On Writing" and Anne Lamott's " Bird by Bird." You can also check out blogs like ProBlogger (Darren Hardy owns this blog where lots of useful information is shared).

Dissect specific aspects of writing that you enjoy and aspire to do

It is where practicing mindful reading takes effect. It's not enough to just read; you also need to pay attention to how the author made the book remarkable.

Here's a practical exercise you can do immediately to hone your craft and stir up your creativity simultaneously.

Go to Amazon, select the category you are writing for in the Kindle Books section, and pick the Best Sellers that catch your eye. Now do a little more digging by going into the sub-category you're writing in and collect a sample size of at least five books out of the top ten. Be meticulous in choosing those top five then read all samples.

Here's a question you want to answer when done reading. Did the first line hook me? If yes, why? If no, why not? And if you did get hooked, how did the author manage to do it? You also want to take note of the books that made you want to keep reading and ask yourself what the author did to stimulate that urge in you. Could you already figure out the viewpoint of the main character? How did you feel about him or her? Why were you able to connect with the character so much?

Now that you've done this practical exercise, it's time to reflect on your work in progress. Are there elements you can incorporate into your book as well? What new ideas are coming up? And just like that, you're back in the original game.

Conduct an in-depth analysis of a book or a blog

All good writers create stories that are well organized and understandable, so when analyzing a book, here are a few pointers. Start with the characters. Get to know who the main characters are, their biases, what their roles are in the unfolding of the story, etc. Then carefully look at the events, what happens in the story, and ask yourself why the events play out as they do. Can you easily figure out the theme, setting, and whether any symbolism has been used? How is the story organized? What is the writing style of the author? Is the writing richly detailed or sparse? Be sure to take lots of notes as you go through this exercise.

How I Recommend Putting all this Together

I know it can be daunting (after gathering all this knowledge), knowing how to make it work for you. So, here's an overview of how I've developed my writing system keeping in mind that it's still work in progress too.

Researching and assembling my materials

On average, I am reading three books on various topics at any given moment. I also research online for comments and articles around the given topic I want to write. I read first thing in the morning and also make it a priority to read the last thing at night.

As I find interesting ideas, I highlight them or use my Evernote if it's online. Here's where I like to mine for gold when it comes to my writing.

1. I subscribe to multiple writers' email lists and also have a list that I continue to update of authors or books I want to read.

2. As I do the dishes every evening or other household duties, I am actively listening to audiobooks, podcasts, or other audio content.

When it comes to collecting all my materials in an organized place, I am a sucker for Evernote if it's online or the good old highlighter pen. I also have a notes app on my iPad, which is very handy as I can jot down notes as soon as they come to me. If I am outdoors and can't access my app, I email myself the ideas. I am also creating a swipe file folder where I am saving URLs of fascinating articles and web pages on the various topics I write.

Finally, when it comes to writing and honing my craft, I do my best to keep things super simple. I write around the same time every day, even on weekends and holidays. Currently, my daily goal is 1,000 words, but I want to work that up to 2,500 in each sitting. Music is essential to my writing. Without it, nothing of value gets accomplished. If, while writing a new and unrelated idea comes to me, I don't just ignore it. Instead, I note it down on my app so I can assess it later, and I have trained myself to stick to that writing until I reach my daily goal come what may. Most days I find that I can even continue with my story past the 1,000-word count, but I stop myself while I'm still hot because I realized (having taken the lesson from Hemmingway) that if I stop while I'm still productive, getting back into it the next day is super easy. It is how I have managed to go a long time without any writer's block. To top it off, honing my skills isn't just about the daily writing, it has also become about reading books on writing. I do my best to analyze novels from authors I like. I can assure you, however, that every writer is different in his or her approach. So, if what I'm doing doesn't feel right for you, that's perfectly fine. This book is a guideline to help you develop a system that works for you and prevents you from falling into the dreaded writer's block.

I want you to write your system following the steps I wrote and clearly state how you will gather your resources, how and when you will write, and what you will do to start developing your skills. Be as detailed as possible; print it out and hang it where you can see it until it becomes the only way you work. Of course, you may not always be able to follow the detailed document to a tee when life gives you some unexpected curveballs. But having that written document will enable you to bounce back and figure out any leaks that need fixing.

Finding a Big Enough Motive to Jump-Start Your Writing and Get You Unstuck

While we writers love what we do, no one said this path would be easy. This uphill struggle that you feel stuck in is something every writer is very familiar with, so why do we do it? What drives us to keep going even in the face of rejection, self-doubt, loneliness, and oh yes, writer's block?

If your mind wants to do anything but write and you're wondering how you will ever finish your project, this is an excellent time to take a step back and remind yourself of what keeps you passionate about your writing.

Perhaps for you, the driving factor is sharing your wisdom, knowledge, and story with the world. Maybe you have a desire to give people the benefits of the experiences you've had, the places you've been, the people you've met, and the things you've seen and done.

There's nothing more satisfying in the world than the hope that our writing has touched even a single person and made their life better. Whether it's to motivate the person to make a change, to inspire them to keep persevering and achieve goals, to help heal a broken heart, or to help a reader move on, let go, shed a tear, smile, or laugh out loud. The fact that we can produce words that people can relate to at that deeper level is one of the most significant driving factors behind most writers, including myself. So, what is truly driving you to write this book? Surely if you can honestly answer that question within yourself, the next steps and your new words typed out shall begin to take form in your mind. Whether you now realize this fully or not, the same mind is lost for words; it's the same mind that holds the finished blueprint of your book. Seek no further than your own mind to help find the words needed to reach your goal successfully.

CONCLUSION

You've received encouraging words from various writers whose advice I've added in this book as well as my struggles, strategies, and systems all aimed at showing you that you can overcome writer's block. It can be very discouraging to feel stuck, but as Maya Angelou pointed out at the beginning, we must be careful not to give too much power to the realization that there's a block preventing us from doing what we love. As long as you don't give up on your writing and finishing your project, you will overcome it. Find creative ways to inspire yourself, test every tip, suggestion, and strategy outlined in this book. Keep yourself accountable, and do not forget to reconnect with your why. Remind yourself why you got into writing in the first place and why this current book needs to be finished and published.

When you finally do summon your muse and start writing again, release the past, forgive yourself, and don't feel guilty for falling behind. The lost creativity and inspiration will come back, and, as soon as it pours in, make sure you reflect to see where you can improve and the support structures you can set up to make sure you prevent this from happening in the future. Remember that writing system we touched on earlier?

Now is the time to start creating it. Put this book down, open a new document, and start building your first system for writing. It is one of the secret ingredients that will ensure your writing career gets better with time.

RESOURCES

Chapter 6, Sleep on it, page 51-53:
Tuck. "Creativity and Sleep" Jan 9, 2020,
https://www.tuck.com/creativity-and-sleep/
Jan 10, 2020.

Chapter 5, Increasing Your Productivity, page 39-40:
Deci, Edward L. "Why We Do What We Do: Understanding Self-Motivation" Aug 1, 1996,
https://www.amazon.com/Why-We-WhatUnderstanding-Self-Motivation/dp/0140255265 Jan 11, 2020.

Chapter 5, Tips on How to Manage Your Energy, page 36-37:
Chopra, Deepak. "Super Brain: Unleashing the Explosive Power of Your Mind to Maximize Health, Happiness, and Spiritual Well-Being" Nov 6, 2012, https://www.amazon.it/Super-Brain-Unleashing-Explosive-Well-Being/dp/0307956830 Jan 11, 2020

Chapter 3, Read a book on writing, page 65:
King, Stephen. "On Writing: A Memoir of the Craft" Oct 3, 2000,
https://www.amazon.co.uk/Writing-Memoir-Craft-Stephen-King/dp/1444723251
Jan 10, 2020

What Did You Think of Writer's Block?

First of all, thank you for purchasing this book, The Journey to Overcoming Writer's Block. I know you could have picked any number of books to read, but you picked this book and for that I am extremely grateful.

I hope that it added value and quality to your writing life. If so, it would be really nice if you could share this book with your writing friends, family and community by posting to **__Facebook__** *and* **__Twitter__**.

If you enjoyed this book and found some benefit in reading it, I'd like to hear from you and hope that you could take some time to post an honest review. I value my readers feedback as gaining exposure as an independent author relies mostly on word of mouth reviews and this would greatly improve my writing craft for future projects and make this book even better. So, if you have the time and inclination, it would be much appreciated if you could leave a review at your place of purchase.

I wish you all the best in your future success!

About the Author

Roger Willis is an established writing coach with the view to help people write from conception to the final manuscript. For over ten years, he is considered a trusted coach with immense knowledge. He has helped hundreds of talented writers unlock their creativity and writing skills, embrace the right mindset, and tackle writer's block; through to successfully publishing and marketing their writing crafts.

Roger lives in North Carolina, USA, with his wife and two children. He studied an MSc degree in Psychology and spent his previous working life as a Teacher before following his passion for writing and became a full-time author and coach in 2010.

He has a love for traveling with his family and reading thriller and sci-fi/fantasy books. He's an avid table tennis player and considers himself quite the wine tasting expert.

Roger is also the author of Write Your Book Today. He has also written sci-fi and fantasy books under several pen names. He's currently writing more self-help books to help writers across the world to follow their passion and master the art of writing – watch this space.

BABY TO TODDLER

TODDLER

A SIMPLE GUIDE FOR NEW PARENTS

Elizabeth Armstrong

Disclaimer: This book is for general guidance only. To the best of our knowledge all advice and care given is correct at time of publishing but ideas and information have a way of evolving and so can change. If there are any medical concerns then that is beyond the remit of this book and guidance should be sought from your General Practitioner (GP) or other health professional.

Table of Contents

Introduction

"Nothing better than spending an entire morning staring into my baby daughter's eyes whispering, I can't do this." - Ryan Reynolds

This quote from famous actor, Ryan Reynolds, provides great insight into what many new parents feel when they bring home their bundle of joy. He also said he had yet to meet a new parent who hasn't experienced this feeling. This new challenge of parenting can be filled with feelings of happiness and joy but may also be intimidating and cause you to feel overwhelmed or anxious.

The main challenge that new parents encounter is adjusting to the complete change of life's routines and priorities. The joyful anticipation of family life can sometimes be overshadowed by negative emotions, fears and anxiety. This may include resenting the loss of your personal freedom, self-doubt about being a good parent and anxiety about additional financial responsibilities.

If you feel this way, don't despair! Parenthood is an emotional and complex endeavour that will bring out a range of emotions in you. This is understandable. You are now responsible for a tiny new life that is completely dependent on you. Other than crying, a baby can't communicate what they want or how they feel. This is bound to be stressful!

Nature has already instilled in you the natural instincts and skills required to love, protect and nurture your child. Knowing this should give you comfort and confidence. You can do this!

As you embark upon this grand new adventure of raising a child, you may have questions about the day to day challenges you may face, and wish you had a concise guide as to what to expect in the next two years.

This book offers practical information combined with simple strategies and tips to help you cope with the challenges you will face as a new parent. The book will address challenges like postpartum depression, loneliness, sleep deprivation and the many changes that come with parenthood. We will share with you the importance of self-care and give you some techniques you can use to improve your sense of personal wellbeing. We will outline what to expect in terms of milestones as the baby grows from a new-born into a toddler. You can also expect to learn:

- How to prepare yourself and your home for the arrival of a new-born
- Developmental changes and common challenges for babies in each age group
- How to adapt to your changing roles and relationship
- Effective parenting techniques
- Age appropriate activities

In this book, we also anticipate your most pressing questions and concerns and give you sound answers and advice. This valuable information will help you ensure your child's healthy development through infancy to becoming a toddler.

It is natural to have concerns about providing the best for your new baby. The first few weeks and months of new parenthood can be fraught with conflicting emotions as you adjust to your new routine and the responsibility of raising your child.

Empowering yourself with the best possible information will give you the tools you need to provide the best possible start for your baby while helping you get the most enjoyment out of the experience. As you learn more about your baby and yourself you will improve and refine your parenting process. As you successfully provide for your baby's needs, you will develop a deep and lasting bond. This deep bond between parent and child is one of the greatest joys of parenthood!

We look forward to being with you on your new journey and helping you to navigate some of the inevitable challenges you will face.

Chapter One: The Basics

"Let choice whisper in your ear and love murmur in your heart: Be ready. Here comes life." - Maya Angelou

Before you bring your new baby home, there are many preparations to make. Preparing for your baby has two aspects: mental and physical.

Mental Preparation

Mental preparation entails getting yourself in the right state of mind to receive the baby.

This means empowering yourself by learning what to do when you go into labour and what to do to take care of your baby's needs upon arrival. When parents are mentally prepared they are able to make the best decisions on a daily basis and are ready if any emergencies occur.

Preparing mentally for childbirth also improves your experience. The basics of mental preparation before the baby comes include banishing negative self-talk. Tell yourself that you can do this rather than indulging self-doubt. Avoid watching or listening to horror stories about labour. This will help reduce your fear. Women have been doing this for thousands of years. You can too!

Preparation includes a birth plan. The birth plan communicates your wishes and preferences for the birthing process to your caregivers. This allows you to have some control over your experience and have a say in the decision making about the options available to you. The birth plan can also include the care you want for yourself during labour and delivery, and the care you want for your baby in the first few days in the hospital.

A good birth plan has the following information accessible to the care team:

- The address of the hospital you are supposed to go to
- Your doctor's name and contacts
- Names and contacts of your support system, including your birthing partner, parenting partner, next of kin or your midwife if you have one
- Pain management options including medication or massages
- Your blood type and any health conditions you may have
- Preferred delivery options
- Feeding plan including instructions about breastfeeding or formula use
- The atmosphere you prefer including music, TV or complete silence
- Whether you will allow videos/photos of the birth

These are some of the basics of a good birth plan, but you can add whatever information you feel is relevant.

Physical Preparation

Nesting is the desire to perfectly prepare your home for the new-born. It is a natural instinct that new parents experience. This includes cleaning, organising and planning well in advance of the baby's arrival. This form of physical preparation will help relieve pressures following childbirth.

This is because you have anticipated your needs and ensured that you will have what you need. You may have prepared meals, stocked the pantry, washed and organised the baby's clothes and arranged for postpartum care in advance.

Important Aspects Of Physical Preparation

<u>*Cleaning*</u>

Wash all the baby's items and organize them according to size and frequency of wear. You also need to clean the entire house and address any issues like mould and mildew. Studies have shown that mould can cause babies to have recurrent wheezing episodes in their infancy and develop allergies later in life. A thorough cleaning of the house and its contents is important for the health and safety of the baby.

<u>*Stock Up*</u>

Buy enough food for at least two weeks to a month or longer if you can afford to. This is so that you don't have to worry about leaving the house for groceries. This is especially important if you are a single parent. Stock up on nutritious and healthy foods that will help restore your body back to health, and make sure to sneak in a treat for yourself.

You should also stock up your medicine cabinet. Ensure that you have baby paracetamol and a thermometer in the house. You will also need something for nappy rash and some nipple cream for your breasts. The nipple cream comes in handy if you experience cracked nipples because of the baby's constant sucking. You may also need some pain relief medicine for the first few days because of the childbirth. Make sure to consult with your doctor about what medicine is safe to take when you are breastfeeding.

Practice

Practice makes perfect. There are several things you can practice before the baby comes. How to carry the baby in a body sling or baby carrier is one of them. Practice placing the baby in the sling using a teddy bear. Since your baby is quite fragile, placing the baby in the sling is a delicate affair and baby carriers can be tricky especially for first time parents. You can also use the teddy bear approach to learn how to strap your baby into their pram, stroller or car seat. When the baby comes home you will have confidence handling them and their specialized gear since you have already practiced using it safely.

Organise

Talk to family members and friends about what help they might be able to provide to you and make a list. Organise a tentative schedule that shows when people can come over to help you and make lists of things you will need help with.

Create a list of emergency contacts. The contacts should include local emergency numbers, your OB/GYN, family members, your parenting partner and service providers that are important to you, such as utilities. Create a separate list of people you would like to notify once the baby is born.

Make a list of things you can't afford to mess up! For example, have a schedule of bills that need to be paid no matter how distracted you are with the baby.

Make Relevant Arrangements

Make the relevant arrangements for maternal and paternal leave if applicable. This is an important part of ensuring your financial stability going forward. It is best to take care of these arrangements before the baby comes so that you can concentrate on having and taking care of the baby. If you are unsure of your exact dates, fill out the parts of the form that you can and submit it. The remaining sections can be filled in after the baby has arrived.

Create A Parenting Schedule

If you have a parenting partner, work together to create a tentative parenting schedule that takes into account each other's needs and strengths. For example, since mum needs to focus on feeding, mum's parenting partner can take over other tasks like washing the baby clothes, preparing meals or running errands.

Support Systems Outside The Core Family Unit

Before the baby comes, you will have time to research what support you may be able to access from people outside your core family unit. This is especially important if you are a single mother with little family support.

Play Groups

Infants benefit from social play. This helps them grow in their interpersonal skills and also helps with their developmental milestones. As infants play with each other their abilities tend to grow more as they spend more time on the activity and see each other doing things.

These groups encourage physical activities and allow babies to enjoy their imagination. Play groups can be free or have fees and they are just as beneficial to parents as they are to children. The open-ended play structure helps parents relax and learn to appreciate the growth and development in their babies. It also gives you the chance to interact with other adults and connect with those on a similar path.

Nannies

Nannies are professional caregivers who provide a safe, nurturing environment for the baby to grow and thrive. They sometimes play a part in making decisions concerning the infant. This kind of assistance to the mother may include creating a daily schedule of activities, grocery shopping and transporting the baby to doctor's appointments. Some nannies live with the family while caring for the baby's needs. The role of the nanny is much more involved than that of a babysitter. A nanny may sometimes act as a surrogate parent when the parent is not as available as they would like to be.

Babysitters

Babysitters are different from nannies because they are not involved in regular day to day care for the baby. They tend to be occasional child care providers. Their main role is to take care of the baby for a few hours under the direction of the baby's primary caregiver. While they are with the baby, they are responsible for their health and wellbeing. Typical duties assigned to the babysitter include playing with the baby, changing nappies, preparing baby food, feeding the baby, and putting the baby to bed.

Essential Must Have Items for Your New-born

Baby Cot

To ensure safety when your baby sleeps, it is important to choose the right sleeping options. For most parents, the ideal first bed for a baby is a "Moses basket". This is a great option while the baby is still tiny because mum can carry it or move it around when needed, and the baby is safe because they can't pull themselves up or roll out of it yet.

Soon they will outgrow this little basket style bed and need something larger and stronger like a baby cot. When choosing a cot, consider the space available in your home, portability, construction materials, storage and design. Always choose a cot that meets safety standards.

The best baby cots have adjustable heights. This allows you to move the base of the cot up or down. When the baby is still small you may need the base to be up high so that you have easy accessibility. As they grow older, they are able to hold on to the rails and pull themselves up. You can drop the base of the cot down so that it is deeper and they can't get out. A cot with three height adjustments and drop-down sides is standard.

Choose a cot with safe plastic coverings on the rails. Any other material can hurt the baby when they bite the railings. The plastic coverings are also essential for protecting the cot and increasing longevity. If you travel often with your little one, consider a travel cot that is easy to move around with. Travel cots are lightweight and come in interesting designs like pop-up and tent-like styles.

Parents should look for the following features and standards in the cot they buy:

- Slatted sides which are strong
- Storage features like drawers
- Nappy changing section
- BSI number (number signifying that the cot meets safety standards)
- The option of matching furniture for the cot
- Wheels on the cot allowing you to move the unit

Baby Mattress

It is a great idea to get a cot and mattress at the same time. This way you can ensure the mattress is the correct fit. To eliminate hazards, like the baby's foot or hand getting stuck between the mattress and cot, the mattress must properly fit the cot. There are three choices of baby mattresses: foam, innerspring and organic.

- Foam mattresses: These are the lightest option and they come in different thicknesses. The best ones are firm and thick offering excellent support for the baby's delicate neck.
- Innerspring mattresses: These are spring mattresses that are coated with foam and padding for cushioning and support. They are very durable since the springs are heavy gauge steel. Your baby can use this mattress for a long time. The innerspring mattresses are usually more expensive than foam mattresses.
- Organic: If you are concerned about toxins, organic mattresses are an excellent choice. They are made from natural materials like coconut fibres and husks, wool, cotton, natural latex and plant polymers. These mattresses are the most expensive of the three options but they are free of toxic components, and babies have less allergic reactions from organic products. Mattresses have been found to contain flame retardants and chemicals like benzene which cause brain development disorders and are carcinogenic.

Some mattresses have removable covers that can be machine washed. Ensure that you also invest in a durable mattress cover. These covers extend the life of your baby mattress and prevent the mattress from getting filthy over time.

Fitted Sheets

Fitted sheets for the baby cots are a great option. These come with elastic edges that fit perfectly around the mattress and are strong enough to stay on despite the baby's movements. Some come with zippers to keep the sheet fastened. They come in cotton and polyester. Opt for sheets that have been pre-shrunk to guarantee that the sheets will still fit after washing.

Nursing Equipment

As a new mum, nursing will take up a lot of your time for the next year! Having the right tools at your disposal makes it easier and more pleasant.

- **Feeding bottles with teats:** Whether you are planning on breastfeeding or using baby formula, you will need feeding bottles.
- **Burp cloths:** After feeding, the baby needs to be burped, and you need a cloth on your shoulder or it will be all over your clothes.
- **Breast pump:** Breastfeeding mothers can express milk using a breast pump so that it can be stored for later use.
- **Storage containers:** You will need containers to store the milk after using the breast pump.
- **Nursing bras:** The cup of these bras open at the front using Velcro, so you can breastfeed more conveniently. Nursing bras should be a size bigger

than your pregnancy bra to accommodate your breasts being swollen up with milk.

- **Breast pads:** Breast pads are excellent for hiding embarrassing breast milk leakages. Wear them with a nursing bra.
- **Nursing pillow:** One of the most underestimated nursing items is the nursing pillow. A nursing pillow helps mum maintain the right posture during breastfeeding. This eliminates issues like back problems caused by bending over to feed the baby. The pillow elevates the baby which brings the infant closer to the breast, supporting their head and neck in the process.
- **Nipple cream:** Your nipples can become sore from the baby's pulling and sucking. Use nipple cream to soothe you between feeds. Nursing experts also recommend applying some breast milk on the nipples to help the healing process.
- **Bottle washing brush:** It is really important to keep your bottles clean!
- **Formula:** Your doctor will most likely recommend breastfeeding, but not everyone can breastfeed. If this is the case for you, the next best thing is formula. Buy only enough to last a week or two. This allows you to test the product before you invest in more. Some babies are allergic to some formulas. The American Academy of Paediatrics advises that babies who are not breastfed should be on formula that contains iron.
- **Thermal bottle carrier:** This keeps the infant bottles warm or cool. They are an essential item when you are using feeding bottles. Choose a thermal bottle carrier that has a stable base to keep the bottles on a level surface to prevent spillage. Make sure the carrier can keep the bottles warm or cold for a long period of time.

- **Bibs:** The baby will spit up while they are nursing. This will help keep them clean.
- **Steam steriliser:** A steam steriliser is essential for keeping the baby's bottles germ free. Choose a steam steriliser that is easy to clean, cools down rapidly, dries bottles thoroughly and has a quick sterilisation cycle. It should be able to sterilise multiple bottles simultaneously. We recommend units that are easy to operate and are constructed with safe materials like BPA-free plastic. Modern sterilisers use UV light to kill germs. Alternatively you can use a sterilising solution or tablets to sterilise bottles using cold water. The solution is viable for 24 hours and the bottles can be ready for use within 15 minutes.

Nappy Changing Essentials

You have the option to use disposable or reusable nappies. Both options come in different sizes to accommodate your baby's size and growth. Buy several dozen at a time because your little one will be going through them quickly! Until they are about a month old, new-borns go through 10 to 12 nappies a day. Since they are only drinking milk or formula, they urinate after almost every meal. They also have three or four bowel movements daily.

Cloth Reusable Nappies Versus Disposable Nappies

- **Comfort:** Cloth nappies and disposable nappies have the same level of comfort. The secret is making sure that you remove the nappy as soon as it is soiled. Neither option is comfortable when it is full. However, disposable nappies can contain chemicals that react with the baby's skin.

- **Price:** The initial investment of cloth nappies will cost more than disposable ones, but there are many options available, from buying new to buying second hand and also the subsequent use of them with siblings that come along in the future. If you consider the average amount of nappies used over a 2 and half year period, reusables will be roughly over 4 times cheaper.
- **Convenience:** Disposable nappies are considered more convenient because you can throw them away after use. They are also more absorbent and the waist and legs have waterproof bands to prevent leaks.
- **Environment:** Disposable nappies have a bigger impact on the environment. It will take roughly 200 - 500 years for the disposable nappy to decompose. These are not small numbers! Whereas, disposable nappies use trees and plastic, cloth nappies use water and energy to wash. Disposable nappies fill up landfills, however cloth nappies only release dirty water with detergent.
- **Safety:** If you choose reusable nappies, you will need to use safety pins or Velcro bands to fasten them. It is recommended to use the Velcro bands over safety pins for safety reasons. The safety pin can spring open and hurt the baby.

Here is a handy list of other essential nappy changing supplies you should have:

- **Changing pad:** A changing pad is what you change the baby on. To keep everything - especially the baby - clean and safe, always change nappies on a changing pad.

- **Waterproof covers:** To keep the changing pad clean and hygienic, waterproof covers for your changing pad are essential. Be careful about what type of plastic the cover is made from. Avoid PVC/vinyl since it is a carcinogen. This plastic is softened using toxic materials such as phthalates that are linked to asthma, kidney and liver problems and cancer. PEVA is not as toxic as PVC but use it with caution. The material also contains chemicals which can leak into the air. Polyurethane is the safest plastic option for waterproof covers.

- **Wipes and washcloths:** Unscented baby wipes are essential to wipe your little one clean after they have a bowel movement. Some parents prefer using a washable cloth with some baby soap and water. Since baby wipes are not biodegradable and can take over 100 years to decompose, many parents are opting for reusable washcloths.

- **Nappy rash cream:** One of a parent's most dreaded sights is seeing an angry nappy rash on their baby. Don't worry! Nappy rash is common and it is easy to treat. You can apply some nappy rash cream and it will clear up within a day or two. After applying the cream, let your little one stay without a nappy on for a while. A little air will help with the healing process and babies love the freedom. Keeping your baby's bottom clean and dry is the secret to preventing nappy rash.

- **Nappy bag:** Of course, you will need a nappy bag to carry all your baby changing supplies around if you go out! The best nappy bag is one that is easy to carry with lots of room for storing baby's essentials. Consider one with insulated pockets for feeding bottles and a foldable changing pad. Also, make sure it is easy to clean and has stroller clips so that you can conveniently attach the bag to the stroller. There are three popular types of nappy bags: tote bag, backpack and messenger.

Bath Essentials

- **Baby bathtub.** The most common options are either in-sink or basin style. The in-sink bathtub is ideal for new-borns. It fits right inside or over the sink and is made of materials like mesh, cloth and plastic. These bathtubs are collapsible for easy storage. The basin bathtub can sit in a traditional bathtub or on the floor. This bathtub has a stopper to let the water out when needed. For the first year this is a great bathtub to use. You can also use a traditional tub with baby friendly inserts that create adjustable recline positions for the baby during bath time. This can be used until the baby becomes a toddler.
- **Wash cloths and sponges:** Use soft cloths and sponges for washing the baby.
- **Baby shampoo, body wash or soap:** Parents have a wide range of choices when it comes to baby body washes, shampoos, soaps and lotions. You can choose from organic products, tear free shampoos and unscented or scented products. Did you know that baby shampoo can work like a body wash too?
- **Hooded towels:** Once the baby is out of the water you need to have a towel handy. Hooded towels are recommended because they allow you to swaddle the baby from head to toe keeping the baby warm before they get dressed. These towels are soft against the baby's sensitive skin.

- **Baby lotion:** Baby lotions help lock in their skin's moisture and help with dry skin. Since some children are sensitive to synthetic fragrances, using a natural unscented option is ideal.
- **Hair brush:** Use a very soft brush that is made for babies.

Wardrobe Essentials

- **Undershirts and t-shirts:** This is a little shirt that can be worn when running around in nappies or with any pants, shorts or skirts.
- **Onesies (one-piece pyjamas - long and short sleeved):** Onesies are essential for everyday use. They are comfortable and easy to put on the baby. At home and in warm weather, these are the best clothing items. When shopping for a new-born make sure that you buy the same item in different sizes to accommodate the baby's growth spurts.
- **New-born hats:** Babies lose a lot of heat from their head. Soft caps are excellent for cold months and wide brimmed baby hats work for hotter months.
- **Pants, shorts, skirts or dresses:** The baby will grow very fast, so don't buy too many.
- **Jackets and cardigans:** Dress the baby warmly for the cold weather.
- **Socks/booties:** Always protect the baby's feet and keep them dry and warm.
- **Scratch mittens:** Scratch mittens are essential to prevent the baby from scratching themselves and you with their fast growing little nails.
- **Bunting bags/swaddlers:** These make the baby feel warm, cosy and snug. The blanket material needs to have some elasticity to fit snugly around the baby

while still remaining breathable. These will keep the baby warm if you are carrying them outside. They are also great for putting the baby down to sleep.

- **A few "fancy" outfits (rompers are ideal):** You may be wondering why so few dress up outfits have been recommended. This is because your baby is going to outgrow them quickly, and the baby is mostly indoors for the first few months or so. You will only use a dress up outfit for photos or special outings, so you may prefer to buy it directly before an event to ensure it fits.
- **Baby friendly laundry detergent:** When washing the baby's laundry, use gentle laundry detergent that is easy on the baby's skin. Remember, the baby is very sensitive to harsh scents and chemicals.

Baby Gear

- **Baby monitor:** Monitors are available in audio and audio/video models. A video monitor is also known as a baby cam. These small devices allow you to hear and/or see what your baby is doing in their nursery. If your baby sleeps in a separate room, this can be an effective way to keep tabs on your baby while enjoying a bit of freedom in your home. Some monitors have advanced technology to help keep your baby safe. For example, temperature detection to help monitor the temperature in the baby's room, or a talk back feature that allows you to talk to your baby from another room. Others come with music and lullabies to soothe the baby or light displays that entertain the baby. A remote control allows you to switch these features on and off when you need to.

- **Stroller/Pram:** Strollers and prams help you move around outside the home with your baby without having to carry them in your arms. You can go out for longer and the baby can get some fresh air and sun. A full-size stroller or pram is the best option. It should have a comfortable seat, expandable canopies, storage areas and even snack trays and cup holders. They can be bulky so you need adequate space for storage both at home and in the car.
- **Car seat:** A car seat is another essential item for babies. Choose a car seat that will accommodate the baby as they grow. Convertible car seats can be used with a new-born as a rear facing car seat, converted into a front facing seat as the infant grows and then into a booster when they are older. Most importantly, make sure you buy one that conforms to the latest safety standards. Age, weight and height are all factors you will need at your disposal.
- **Baby carrier:** As you move around you may want to strap your baby to you using a baby carrier that frees your hands so you can do other things. The carrier is easier to use in crowded places and it can also be more comfortable. You can even use it to carry the baby around in the house. It is also easy to work with and they are designed to be a good fit to the parent's body.
- **Play pen:** This is a soft enclosure place where you can put the baby to play with their toys so they are safe when you are doing something else.
- **Baby bouncer:** Babies love to bounce and this keeps them safe while they explore being upright. This keeps your hands free to do other things.
- **High chair:** A high chair becomes essential when you begin introducing the infant to solid food. Opt

for a high chair that can be used from infancy to toddlerhood. Ease of cleaning and adjustability are some of the qualities to look for in a high chair.

- **Pacifiers (or dummies):** Pacifiers can be useful to soothe the baby and they may even help the baby fall asleep, but you don't need a pacifier to soothe your baby all the time. Babies can become dependent on the pacifier for self-soothing which is a habit you will have to break later.

First Aid Kit

The first aid kit for babies should include a toothbrush, nail clippers, blunt scissors, medicine droppers, nasal aspirator, baby thermometer, bulb syringe and cotton balls. You need petroleum jelly for scabs, as well as antiseptic and bandages for cuts and scrapes. Additional items in the kit include saline drops, antibiotics and infant pain relief medication and gas drops (aka gripe water). These items will make it easier to keep up with baby's personal care and treat any little scrapes they may get.

Musical Mobile

A musical mobile is a great addition to the nursery. It helps keep the baby occupied and soothes them to sleep. Mobiles also provide visual and mental stimulation for the baby which promotes brain development. Introduce a mobile to the baby's sleep environment after about 3-4 weeks. This will allow the baby to adjust to their new environment before adding extra stimuli.

Food Processor

A food processor is a convenient way to puree the baby's food during the weaning period. It is also a great way for you to make nutritious smoothies and soups for yourself. It is possible to puree your baby's food without using a processor, so this is not an essential item, but it is a desirable item.

The Birth: What To Expect

If you have prepared mentally and physically and have acquired all the essential baby supplies, you are ready for the next phase of your journey. Let's go over what you can expect during childbirth.

Signs Of Labour

Your due date is only a reference point for the doctor and yourself to use for planning purposes. The actual date for the birth of your baby may vary by three weeks before or two weeks after the due date.

Lightening: This is the dropping of your baby's head into your pelvis right before delivery. This makes your belly look bottom heavy and you have more need for urination.

Bloody show: This is discharge from your cervix in the form of a brownish-red mucus plug. Seeing this doesn't mean you are automatically going into labour. It can show up a few days before labour or can come right before labour begins. Loose stool is another sign that labour is imminent.

Amniotic fluid: The phrase "my water broke" means that the fluid contained in the amniotic sac has been released from the membranes that protect it. This fluid protects your baby and when it comes gushing out, your baby is ready to come. Once you see this fluid you will go into labour within the next 24 hours. Sometimes labour doesn't come even after the water breaks. As a result, the doctors may induce labour, however it is always a good idea to contact your midwife when this happens for advice.

Contractions: The contractions indicate that you are in active labour. The closer you are to giving birth, the more intense the contractions become. They will also come in shorter intervals. Labour may take 8-15 hours or more depending on the individual.

Caesarean (c-section): Mothers who are having elective caesarean sections are given a date for the delivery. If you are scheduled for a vaginal delivery and your labour goes on too long, or there are complications, you may be given an emergency c-section. The process of caesarean delivery typically takes about 45 minutes. The baby and mother are then given skin to skin contact just like after a vaginal delivery.

Pain: You can manage the pain of labour and delivery using techniques learned in your birthing classes, if you had access to them. The birthing classes, often called Lamaze classes, teach expectant mothers what kind of pain to expect, and how to breathe, meditate and work through their pain. These techniques may be used with or without pain medication. Pain medication is also available to you if you have arranged for it in advance.

Trauma After Childbirth

The process of childbirth can be hard and even traumatic, but this trauma is manageable during and after delivery. Trauma is usually treated by professionals. Do not be afraid to ask for help. You are not alone and there are many people who can empathize with the challenge you have faced in childbirth. A traumatic childbirth experience can cause postpartum post-traumatic stress disorder. This is different from postpartum depression.

Mothers with postpartum depression do not have traumatic memories of giving birth. Postpartum post-traumatic stress disorder involves flashbacks of the distressful experience during childbirth. This can be caused by the pain or act of delivery or by a health scare with the baby or mother. This can also be experienced by women who undergo invasive fertility treatments.

You can receive help from health professionals one on one or talk to others in support groups. Remember that you are not alone. Postpartum post-traumatic stress disorder is experienced by 9% of new mothers. Talking to a therapist is very helpful and is the most common treatment women seek for support. Therapies like music, art and dance can also help you cope with the trauma. These artistic expressions allow you to find an outlet for your emotions and separate the trauma from the beautiful gift of your baby.

If you are experiencing ongoing trauma after delivery, online counselling can help for the first few weeks as you heal and are housebound. However, as soon as you are able to, make an appointment with a local therapist. Why is this important? You will find that it is often more effective to have face to face contact with your therapist as you can feel more connected and engaged than when talking to someone on phone or screen. In addition, when you leave the house, you see life going on around you and it injects vitality into your life. The fresh air and the change of scene will do wonders for your state of mind. Staying indoors will only make you feel more isolated.

Remember, you are unique so your healing will be unique to you. Try various methods to see what works for you. Keep in mind that you are not at fault and do not engage in negative self-talk. Go at your own pace and allow yourself the time to heal.

Common Questions About Preparing For A New-born

When should you start preparing for your new-born?

After you have crossed the first trimester you can begin preparing for the baby's arrival. Doctors consider the first trimester to be between 0 to 14 weeks. According to experts, 80% of miscarriages occur during this period. After the first trimester the chances of a miscarriage drop to between 1-5%.

How can spouses and loved ones prepare for the arrival of the baby?

It is important for mums to have support at all stages of pregnancy, childbirth and child raising. Whether you are a spouse, significant other, loved one, family or friend, make sure that you attend parenting and other classes with the expectant mother. It is very comforting to mum to know she will not be alone, and that you care enough to be there with her.

These prenatal classes will give you insight into what to expect when your little one arrives. These classes also equip you to be physically and emotionally fit to care for your partner and the baby. You can decide together with your partner whether you will be in the delivery room or not. If you are helping with birthing, you will learn all the ways you can help during the labour.

Loved ones can also help with the birth plan and ensure that they understand the wishes of the mother to be.

Also, as you get later into your pregnancy (roughly 18-20 weeks), you are able to tell the gender of the baby which may influence what items you and your loved ones can purchase.

How do I prepare my pet for the baby?

Once the baby arrives, pets can become jealous of them and territorial of you. To make the transition easy for your pet begin by getting them accustomed to babies and kids. You have ample time before the baby arrives to do this.

New parents tend to rely on their previous interactions with their pet to gauge its gentleness; however, even the most gentle dog can become aggressive towards a new addition to the family. Invest in obedience training for your dog or cat even if it has already undergone training before. At home you can play recordings of babies crying to get your pet used to the sound. It is also a good idea to act like you have a baby in the house even before the actual baby arrives. For example, carry a swaddled teddy bear, sing to it, change a nappy and invite the pet to sit with you during these activities. If your pet behaves well, reward it with a treat. If you have friends with kids that are used to pets, arrange to have them come over to get the pets used to small children.

Any changes to the living arrangements of the pet as a result of the baby's arrival should be implemented in advance. This gives the pet adequate time to get used to the new sleeping or feeding schedule. Make sure you take the pet for a medical check-up and update all relevant vaccines. Acquire or create a gate that keeps the pet away from the baby and never leave the pet alone with the baby. You must also not leave the pet's food out in the open where the baby can access it, or where the pet feels they have to protect it. Remember, your pet is a loving creature that you have bonded with, so allow it to have some time with your baby to let their natural bond grow. Once the baby is home, let the dog smell your baby's clothes to get his or her scent. When you arrive home with the baby you can let your pet say a quick hello. Lead the pet to where the baby is and while holding the baby let your pet come closer. All the while, talk to your pet in a gentle tone.

Most importantly, don't neglect your pet just because you have a new baby in the home. Your pet needs your love and support in order to properly adjust to the new arrival.

Chapter Two: Taking Care Of Yourself

"To be a good parent, you need to take care of yourself so that you can have the physical and emotional energy to take care of your family." – Michelle Obama

When you bring your new-born home, it is natural to want to focus all your energy on the baby. You may feel that this is your only option, since they have so many needs and you want to be a good parent. Many new parents report being so focussed on providing for the baby that they can't take the time or don't have the energy for a regular shower, meal or sleep.

It is very important that you take the time and energy to take care of yourself. This is known as self-care. While this applies primarily to the birth mother or primary caregiver, it is important that all those involved with caring for the baby take care of their emotional and physical health first.

What To Expect Postpartum (After The Birth)

For Mums

The period known as postpartum begins right after you have delivered your baby. It lasts about eight weeks. During this period, you will have to address many changes, upheavals and adjustments as a new parent. It is an emotional and physical rollercoaster, but there are warm and exciting moments each day as you enjoy the wonders of your new baby.

It is important to understand what to expect, so that you can manage any fears or anxieties you may have and be ready for the changes that will happen to your body as you recover from pregnancy and delivery. It is critical to be kind to yourself, and to manage your expectations of yourself during this time.

In addition to physical changes after delivery, some mothers experience significant changes to their mental and emotional health. This may include profound sadness, despair or despondency following childbirth. This is called postpartum depression, and it is a real condition that requires medical treatment. If you experience postpartum depression, be sure to get help by contacting your local or registered doctor.

As you adjust to new motherhood, you will learn more and more every day about how to care for your baby and what adjustments are required in your life to accommodate your new baby's routine. This is an ever-evolving situation filled with many new discoveries. Despite some of the challenges, there will be a lot of awe-filled moments as you discover all that motherhood has to offer.

Week 1

If you had a vaginal delivery, you will have what is medically known as perineal soreness. This is just a fancy way to say pain in the vaginal region. You already expected that, so although you are not surprised, you will be happy to know that the pain will dissipate in a few days.

What you may not have expected is the blood and tissue discharge. This is the tissue and blood from the uterus that helped your baby grow while in utero. It will come out for a couple of weeks after you have given birth.

Mothers who have had a caesarean section will have some pain at the site of the incision. Pain medication will help a great deal in mitigating it. If you had a catheter it will have been removed.

Women generally have trouble getting out of bed after giving birth, but it is important to move around a bit and increase your circulation in order to avoid getting blood clots. Don't push yourself too much but do move around as much as is comfortable.

In the first week, specifically on the third day, your progesterone and oestrogen levels drop as the oxytocin and prolactin in your body fluctuates. As a result, mums feel highly emotional which is perfectly normal. Let your emotions out and express yourself without self-judgement.

Pro Tips:

- Use frozen pads on your perineum (the pelvic floor) to ease the pain.
- Gently wash with some warm water after urination.
- You can take doctor prescribed painkillers to help with the pain. Childbirth experts emphasize using only doctor-prescribed medication to ensure you use something that is safe to use if you are breastfeeding.
- To care for your c-section keep the incision site clean and dry and give it fresh air.

- Take your temperature at least four times a day for the first 72 hours to monitor for infections, such as in the kidney or uterine system.

Week 2-5

By the second week you will experience less bleeding, but it is completely normal for it to go on for up to six weeks. The vagina can feel irritated as the perineum begins to heal. If you have sutures in your perineum they will begin to disintegrate. If you had a c-section, the incision will also be itchy as it begins to heal. C-section mothers may still be sore compared to their vaginal birth counterparts.

You will also be feeling some contractions as you breastfeed and the uterus (or womb) continues to move towards resuming its original position. As you approach the fourth week you will feel fewer and fewer contractions. Some women experience sore nipples during breastfeeding. You may also have some days with constipation. This is sometimes caused by pain medicines in your system or by radical changes in diet or stress level.

Pro Tips:

- Make a deliberate effort to move around more. Fresh air and light exercise are invaluable tools for self-care. Even a short walk outside has innumerable benefits.
- Eat a nutritious diet, including foods high in potassium to help with your energy levels. Bananas, spinach, cantaloupe, grapefruit, sweet potatoes and broccoli are great choices.

- It's important to drink plenty of water whilst pregnant as the baby develops in the womb. Maintain hydration by drinking water in regular intervals to support nutrients, assist digestion, yield extra blood, form new tissue, create amniotic fluid, and remove wastes and toxins.
- If constipation is an issue for you, ask for stool softening medication to give you relief.

Week 6-8

By this time, your uterus is finally settling back into its original position, so you may experience some bleeding on and off. The blood is usually bright red but the bleeding will stop in a couple of days. During this time, you can expect your doctor to clear you for more intense activity such as driving and low impact exercise. During this period, and indeed at all times post-delivery, you need to keep vigilant for signs of complications. If you have any concerns please seek professional medical help for advice. These signs can include:

- Bleeding that soaks more than one sanitary pad within an hour and continues through the third day
- Blurred vision
- Large clumps of blood clots
- Fever, chills and clammy skin
- Dizziness and fainting spells

For Parenting Partners

Parenting partners tend to experience the most anxiety in the first week after the baby comes home. This is usually because they have to adjust to the responsibility of a new baby, and this means keeping an eye on both baby and mother to ensure their good health. It may be hard to adjust to the baby getting all of the attention. The change of routine - including sleep deprivation - can have a significant effect on your sense of wellbeing. Mum's partner may feel extra pressure to provide for or protect the new family, and this can be stressful. Self-care is important for parenting partners as well and will make you a more effective parent.

Week 1

Feelings of inadequacy and fear of the unknown can quickly overwhelm a new parent. Consider the first week as a sharp learning curve and don't be too hard on yourself. During this week be supportive and take the time to learn basic skills. This can include providing basic support to the mother, taking care of the basics around the home, holding and soothing the baby, nappy changing and making sure supplies are in place.

Since parenting partners don't experience the physical changes that mothers feel while the baby is growing inside them, it may be hard to understand what the mum is going through. Compassion and patience is critical at this time. During her pregnancy, mum began to make many mental and physical adjustments in preparation for motherhood. She may have become used to a poor sleep routine and physical discomforts such as heartburn or constipation.

Mum is in a better position to understand the discomforts of the baby because she has been through so much discomfort too.

Partners may take longer to adjust to inconveniences such as sleepless nights and a fussy baby. They may not quickly grasp the scope of discomfort a baby may be experiencing or they may get frustrated if the baby cries. The first week is all about adjustment and growth, and it's important to remember to be kind to yourself and to have realistic expectations about your abilities and knowledge.

Pro Tips:

- Eat a healthy diet with emphasis on foods that help reduce anxiety and stress. Eat well balanced meals and eat food like eggs, fatty fish like salmon, yogurt and treats like dark chocolate.
- Talk to other parents about any concerns you have.
- Focus on the joy and love you have for your new baby.

Week 2-5

By this time, the parenting partner is beginning to get used to the new routine. You are able to hold and bottle feed the baby as mum takes a rest, and you are an expert at changing nappies. As you continue to provide basic care to the baby you will become closer and your bond will grow more and more. During this time, be on the lookout for signs of paternal postnatal depression (PPND). This condition is characterized by a never-ending feeling of being overwhelmed and feeling left out as mum and baby bond with each other.

Pro Tips:

- Learn to identify the triggers that cause you stress. This may include the baby crying incessantly, an inconsolable partner and/or additional financial obligations. Once you identify your triggers, you can more effectively address them.
- Find someone like a parenthood counsellor to talk to. Their perspective can be invaluable as you learn to navigate your new roles and responsibilities as a parent.
- Make time to exercise and get fresh air.

Week 6-8

By this time, you are feeling more confident as a partner and can handle increasing responsibilities with child care. This may include taking care of the baby while mum goes out for a short time. You are beginning to feel more grounded and are less foggy and fearful, and you should be enjoying the responsibility of being a new parent.

Pro Tips:

- Begin to make more time for exercise outside the house.
- Strive to spend quality time with your partner, family or friends. Enjoy the simple things like playing a board game, cook together, or just lie on the couch and watch a movie. Maintaining a strong bond between parents is key.

Hindrances To Self-Care

It may seem nearly impossible to prioritize yourself and your needs when you have a new baby in the house. They need so much and so often! However, it is crucial to remember that by making time for self-care, you are acting in the best interests of the baby. New parents often report feeling that the needs of the baby supersede any of their own. These feelings are normal and to be expected; however, it is easier to truly meet the needs of your new-born when you are in good physical and mental health.

To ensure you are able to make time and energy for self-care, identify and address the challenges that may be impacting your ability to prioritize this important activity.

Lack Of Preparedness

Nothing completely prepares you for the change that parenthood brings to your life. As a new parent you may have little experience to draw from, so some fear and apprehension is to be expected. As a result of major changes in your sleep and exercise routine, basic personal care can become a challenge. In some cases, you may be unprepared for the unforeseen financial strain that comes with having a new addition to the family. A lack of preparedness can result in not having the knowledge or tools to properly address the challenges you will face as a new parent.

Pro Tips:

- Learn about what to expect from parenthood. Since you are consulting this book, you have already

48

taken a positive step towards increased preparedness. Good for you! Talk to friends and family about their experience.

- Allow yourself the time to adjust to the changes of your new life without expecting too much of yourself. As you learn more and practice new skills you will become more comfortable.
- Prioritise the care of yourself and your baby over other things like chores.
- It is also okay to put off hosting well-meaning family and friends. Loved ones will understand when you say you are not ready to have company over.

Changes In Roles

The truth is that the arrival of a new-born will result in a shift in the roles and responsibilities of those in the household. The mother is naturally focussed on the needs of the baby and will not have the time or energy to accomplish all the tasks in the home that she normally does. When one parent is dedicated to being the primary caregiver of the baby, the tasks normally completed by them may go undone around the home. At this time, there may be increased anxiety about incomplete tasks, or confusion or resentment about the redistribution of tasks around the home. The lack of a domestic support system to assist with tasks will cause extra stress upon the mother and result in an unhealthy environment for mother and baby.

Pro Tips:

- It is important for you to understand that your role in life will change completely. Embrace this reality and all the good things this new life will bring you.
- If you are used to calling the shots, you have to step back and accept that the baby calls the shots now! That's their role, and yours is to nurture that little life while still taking care of yourself and your other loved ones as best you can.
- Be honest with your partner about what you need from them, even if it means they have to learn to do things that you have previously done for the household.
- Those around the primary caregiver must step in to take care of the mother of the home, and other individuals within it.

Loneliness And Isolation

Caring for a new-born baby is a full-time job. Most new parents find it challenging to be without the normal adult time they previously had with their partners, friends and colleagues. It is inevitable that because of the time and energy spent caring for the baby, the dynamics of your relationships with others will change.

Making time for your partner or other adults in your life can be difficult when you are exhausted from taking care of the baby. This may cause you to feel lonely or isolated. Similarly, your focus on the baby may cause your partner to feel lonely and isolated as well.

Pro Tips:

- Talk to your partner or other adults in your life, even if it is for short periods of time. Communication is essential to building a strong network of support around you. Talking to your partner or others gives you the opportunity to share the awe, excitement and even the fears you may be experiencing. This is an opportunity to share your new memories with others, and to ask for advice and help. Even a few minutes on the phone, video chat or over text can make you feel more connected and less alone.
- Find and attend local playgroups and support groups for new parents. This is an opportunity to mingle with new mums and for your baby to socialize with other babies. Share your experiences and do not be afraid to ask questions or express your struggles as this is a safe space for you and your little one.

Ways To Implement Self Care

As the baby continues to grow, their many needs can often overtake the self-care routines of mum and her partner. Building in opportunities for self-care can result in greater physical and mental health. There are various ways that you can integrate wellness routines into your day. Some of these self-care techniques are discussed below.

Learn The Art Of Meditation

Meditation is an ancient practice that remains relevant today. It includes a number of simple techniques that can be used to relax and free the mind and body of anxiety.

You can choose to practice traditional methods of meditation which entail sitting in a serene environment with eyes closed and emptying your mind of all thoughts. Being aware of everything while focussing on nothing is key to this practice. When you clear your mind of other distractions, you can be present in the moment and a sense of calm comes over the body.

Simpler forms of meditation can be implemented at various times of the day. You can meditate just by focussing completely on the rise and fall of your baby's chest while you breathe deeply.

Breathing

Holding your breath when you feel overwhelmed is a natural human reaction to stress, and this leads to tension build up. You can burst that stress bubble by using deliberate deep breathing routines. When you breathe deeply and exhale purposefully, you release built up tension in the body and mind.

When you are feeling overwhelmed, or are feeling a build-up of stress, take three to five deep breaths. Breathe deeply and slowly through your nose, letting your belly and chest rise and fill with air. Then slowly exhale through the mouth.

Journaling

If you have some quiet time, journaling is a great way for new parents to privately express their feelings. This journal can be for venting about what upsets you, but often it can be more positive to use it to record the good things you want to remember about this time.

A gratitude diary is an example of a positive journal exercise. In this diary, you write down what you are grateful for or good things that happened with the baby or other loved ones. There are a lot of new things going on, and a journal will help you look back and recapture some special memories. The practice of gratitude is excellent for your overall wellbeing. It helps you keep your blessings in perspective, especially when you are having a hard day. Document special moments and read the journal when you need to be uplifted. You might be surprised at how you can use these positive memories to get through hard times!

Music

Babies are not the only ones who benefit from a lullaby! Humming, chanting and singing all have a positive impact on your mood and sense of wellbeing. Take every opportunity to entertain and soothe yourself with any or all these forms of music. Make sure the music is uplifting and has a positive message. Hum or sing while you do your tasks. Sing along to your favourite songs. If you enjoy chanting, find a peaceful, affirmative chant that is powerful for you, such as "May complete health and peace abound in me forever" or even something as simple as saying to yourself "Peace and joy".

You don't have to be alone to include music into your self-care routine. Don't be shy! Baby and other loved ones will benefit from hearing you hum and sing a song or mantra. They might even join in!

Ask For And Accept Help

When someone says, "Let me know if there is anything I can do to help", take them up on it! Let family and friends help you. There is no shame in asking for help with laundry or cleaning. Maybe they can cook a few meals you can put in the fridge or freezer for later. Friends and family are also a great resource for childcare when you need a break or need to sleep.

There are also local organisations that assist new parents. Make a list of organisations in your area and find out what services they offer. Even if you don't need it right away, keep the list so you can obtain help if you need it later. This is especially true for single parents who may not have a support system and need relief to prevent exhaustion.

When there are other adults around, take advantage of the opportunity to get a healthy dose of adult conversation and keep up with current events.

Postpartum depression can be a huge challenge for new parents. You may not know where normal fatigue ends and deep depression begins. If you feel overly depressed or overwhelmed, talk to a professional about your feelings so they can give you the support you need.

Have A Baby Routine

A routine may not sound like a self-care strategy but it actually is. It helps you stay organised and increases your chances of having time for rest and personal activities. Have a routine for babies from the time they wake up to the time you put them down for the night. A routine gives babies a sense of stability. As a result of their predictable environment, they feel safe. Most children learn better with routines in place.

Routines also help infants to form healthy habits related to the time of day, such as eating and sleeping. Living with a well-adjusted baby allows you to make time for other things because you can count on the baby to be sleeping or with another caregiver at that time. This gives you the opportunity to schedule self-care activities such as sleep, exercise and pampering. If you have assistance with childcare, a routine can be even more liberating as there are more chances to schedule time for yourself.

Make Time For Each Other

If you have a spouse or birth partner, it can be hard to make special time together when all your resources and attention is focussed on the baby. An occasional "date" reinforces your bond and affection for each other as adults. When you have a moment of respite from the little one; such as a scheduled nap time or child care opportunity, make plans for yourselves as well so that the chance isn't wasted. Plan for a romantic meal for two, watch a film, or simply spend some time talking with each other. Even a short time together can be meaningful if you really focus on one another!

After giving birth, physical intimacy may be difficult to resume for either physical or emotional reasons. Many women report being more interested in resuming physical intimacy after about three months, but it varies among women. Don't let this deter you from making opportunities to inject loving intimate moments into your new lifestyle. Begin by building your emotional intimacy and don't put too much pressure on yourself.

Taking time to work on your relationship will help maintain a cohesive loving atmosphere around your newborn. As your baby becomes sleep trained, opportunities for intimacy become more available and you can enjoy them without being as distracted.

Have A Sleep Schedule

Most people never imagine they would need to schedule sleep. Many new parents think they will be able to wing it. Unfortunately, this lack of planning guarantees that you will be fatigued and sleep deprived all the time. Scheduling your sleep gives you something to look forward to. When you schedule it, you are more likely to use that time to rest instead of getting distracted by the many tasks you have.

Sleep deprivation can be an ongoing challenge that lasts until the baby starts sleeping through the night. The erratic sleep patterns of the baby causes some parents to sleep in the same room as their babies until they start sleeping through the night. For many this offers a better chance of resting since there is less effort to get up from another room and attend to the needs of the baby.

If you have a partner, working in shifts allows you both to have time to sleep while giving each of you dedicated bonding time with the baby. As your infant grows, the need for scheduled sleep diminishes because you will be back to sleeping mostly regular nights.

Single parents need to have family or friends to help them. Create a list of people who can help you and form a sleep schedule around their ability to help you. When they come to check on you let them care for the baby while you catch a nap. Single parents with the resources can also employ professional nanny services or babysitters.

Agree On Parenting Techniques

Parenting is usually a combined effort. It is crucial for those sharing childcare to agree on the fundamentals about what parenting techniques you use. This is especially important when it comes to things like feeding, discipline and exposure to stimuli such as TV.

When the primary caregivers are in agreement, it lessens the chances of fighting. Fighting is negative for the parties that fight as well as the baby who hears it, or who is then stuck with an angry caregiver. Harmony within the home ensures that your baby is well adjusted and forms healthy emotional references about relationships.

The other reason why it is critical for caregivers to agree on parenting is because babies need consistency and structure. If one caregiver is using a napping and feeding schedule, and the other is not, the baby is likely to be unhappy and unhealthy.

You may wonder why this is a self-care routine. Well, a happy baby is a happy parent! Agreeing on parenting techniques ensures that you avoid the distress that can accompany a baby that is fussy and unhappy. It also ensures that you do not develop resentment for your partner if you feel they are compromising your child rearing goals.

Get Some Exercise

Lack of sleep, physical discomfort and time constraints are valid reasons for new parents to put off exercise. Despite this, it is important to be vigilant about how much time you allow to go by before you get active again. Postnatal experts agree that putting off exercise is actually hurting you. Find ways to inject some exercise into your day, no matter how little it is.

Factors like the mother's age, pre-pregnancy weight, lifestyle and eating habits are all factors that determine how easy it is to lose the baby weight. Women in midlife may already be experiencing midlife weight gain. Because of this, losing the weight after the pregnancy may take longer for them than for younger mothers.

Regardless of age or weight, the secret to exercising is... getting started! Work diligently on a healthy weight loss program that starts slowly and progresses to gradually more strenuous exercise.

A safe and workable progression of exercises for a new mum is presented below. Start with tummy toning and work your way up to weight training or aerobic exercises.

Tummy Toning

New mums can be discouraged by the look of the puffy or saggy baby pouch that remains after delivery. Tummy toning is an easy exercise to do, and you can start doing it within the first few weeks of delivery. It helps to strengthen your stomach muscles and you can do it anywhere, anytime. This exercise will begin toning your belly and restore your upright posture.

How to do it: You can do it sitting down or standing up. Whether you are standing or sitting, keep your back straight and inhale deeply while pushing your diaphragm upwards. During the inhalation, contract the stomach muscles and keep your abs tight. Expel your breath slowly and make sure to relax your muscles gradually as you exhale. This will strengthen your core. As you get stronger, increase the number of contractions and length of time of each contraction.

Kegels

As a result of the amount of pressure and weight put on it during pregnancy, your bladder may be weaker. Kegel exercises strengthen your bladder so that you do not have urine leaks when you laugh, pick up your baby, cough or sneeze, or when you exercise strenuously. Kegels help to get your bladder back to strength and avoid embarrassing episodes of incontinence.

How to do it: Contract your uterine muscles and hold them tightly in that position for an extended period of time. Relax briefly and repeat as many times as you can. Do this at least ten times a day. This exercise can be done during urination, which makes it easy to see if you are improving. Start and stop the flow of the urine by contracting and relaxing the muscles. It is not a good idea to try this too frequently, just occasionally to see how you are improving.

Walking

Walking is excellent for new mums because it helps you get fresh air, clears your thoughts and gives you a whole-body workout without being too strenuous. It is the kind of exercise you can enjoy as your infant grows because you can bring them along. Walking is a low impact aerobic exercise and is a great way to ease back into fitness. Walking will restore your muscle strength, raise your energy, help you lose weight and increase your cardiovascular fitness.

How to do it: Begin with a short leisurely walk around your yard and work your way up to slowly walking around the block. Do this for a few weeks to help you strengthen your body and assess your level of health. Acknowledge pain or discomfort by stopping the exercise for a day or two to rest your body. If the pain persists, see a doctor. By the sixth week you will likely be able to go for longer walks at a faster pace. By the third month, as your muscles become stronger and your body begins to regain stamina, you will be able to go for a slow jog. By the sixth month you will be ready to engage in higher intensity cardiovascular activities.

Weight Training

As your infant grows you need the strength to keep up with their activity levels. They will also become heavier, so you need strength to be able to carry them around. Weight training will also help you lose weight, tighten your core and tone your body. Toning your muscles can also help to relieve some of the pain associated with childbirth, like back pain. Strength training using light to medium weights is a good exercise option and it can be done at home or at a local gym.

How to do it: It doesn't take unending hours in the gym to achieve basic fitness. You can achieve your goals by consistently working out for 30 to 45 minutes a few times a week. It is important to choose safe, effective exercises that don't put too much strain on your body. Mums who are new to exercise should opt for light weights (2-5 kgs) initially. As you grow stronger you can begin using heavier weights. It is important to make sure that you maintain the right form and do the exercises properly. If you are unsure, find a course at your local gym or leisure centre that focuses on new mothers. Don't be shy to ask for tips from the trainer!

Easy Exercises At Home

If you can't leave the house you can still get lots of exercise at home and with your baby nearby. Since you are in the comfort of your home you can fit in small amounts of exercise frequently throughout the day. Make the exercise as rigorous as you are able to and be creative about when to add this important activity into your day.

How to do it: Look for opportunities to be active both when the baby is awake and asleep. For example, you can do quiet exercises like front and side lunges as your baby is napping. Additional exercises that you can do quietly at home include squats and pelvic tilts. You can put your hands on a counter and do side leg lifts and miniature push ups. Do arm curls with weights if you have them. If the baby is awake and in the bouncer you can put on some cheerful music and include more vigorous movements like dancing or riding a stationary bike. By the third month you can increase the intensity of your exercises. If you have a parenting partner, arrange your schedules so that you can dedicate regular time for exercise.

Common Questions About Self-Care

Is self-care selfish?

Self-care is not selfish. It is a critical component of taking care of your mental and physical health. Self-care may make the difference between a healthy parent and a stressed one. When you neglect yourself you are likely to grow resentful of your parenting duties. Sometimes that resentment spills over to your little one. Look at self-care as a preventative measure to avoid burnout.

How do I schedule self-care?

Understandably, new-borns are completely reliant on mum, so a whole day off for her at the beginning will be nearly impossible to achieve. However, by the fourth month, it is possible to schedule a full day away from the baby if you have reliable child care assistance. Scheduling self-care is all about communicating with your parenting partner and other supportive people in your life. If you are a single parent, you will work with the schedule you have set for the baby.

If you are able to, take larger portions of time off to accomplish things that improve your mental and physical health. If you aren't able to, recognize that when your baby sleeps is the best time to fit in some self-care like meditating, exercising or napping.

What are the different kinds of self-care?

Establishing a self-care routine should include physical, mental, emotional, spiritual and even professional activities. Schedule self-care every day. Consider the type of self-care you want for the day and allocate the resources necessary.

- **Physical** self-care includes indulging in activities like bathing, exercise, yoga, nutritious meals or getting a facial.
- **Mental** self-care feeds your mind with enriching activities like reading, art and journaling and time with therapists or support groups.
- **Emotional** self-care involves recognizing and releasing your emotions without guilt and finding ways to bring joy into your days. Find yourself a private spot and cry if you want, watch a show that makes you laugh, or sing a song that makes you feel cheerful.

- **Spiritual** self-care applies to your existential beliefs about the human connection to creation. For some people this includes participation in organized religion. For others it involves communing with nature.
- **Professional** self-care helps you remain relevant in your field while you are on parental leave. Take an online course or touch base with colleagues from work. When you go back to work you will make a smoother transition.

Chapter Three: New-born to Three Months

"Ah babies! They're more than just adorable little creatures on whom you can blame your farts." - Tina Fey

The first three months for the baby are about nursing, sleeping, cuddles, nappy changes and clearly, wind. The more love and skin contact you give to your baby, the more your baby will thrive.

Developmental Expectations

Week 1

Your little bundle of joy looks a bit puffy eyed and wrinkly. While in utero, the baby has been in cramped quarters with fluids. Take those first pictures with enthusiasm as those memories are precious and you will want to look back on these first few days. During the first weeks you will notice that the baby will sleep a lot. They need around 14-17 hours of sleep a day. They will wake up for only two to four hours a day to nurse before resuming their peaceful dreams. Take advantage of the baby's long periods of sleep to get some rest as well.

During this week you will notice that they instinctively turn their head towards anything that touches their face. They then proceed to make suckling sounds. This is a very important reflex, known as the rooting reflex, and it helps the baby with breastfeeding. The rooting reflex is complemented by the sucking reflex which your baby exhibits when you place a finger, nipple or bottle nipple into the baby's mouth. The baby automatically begins to suckle.

The baby will also have the Moro reflex, also known as the startle reflex. This is an instinctive survival reflex which causes the baby to cling on to mummy. The baby will either fling their arms outwards, clench their fingers around yours tightly, or jerk awake when you try to put them down to sleep.

Don't worry if you notice some weight loss in your baby. It is normal for babies to lose weight as they get accustomed to nursing and lose pre-birth fluid weight. You can also expect your baby to receive some injections like the vitamin K and a Hepatitis B injection. Vitamin K helps the baby's blood to clot. All babies are born with low levels of vitamin K and because of the umbilical cord which may ooze blood, this is a crucial injection. The Hepatitis B injection prevents infection of vital organs like the liver; this injection may be given soon after birth if thought to be at risk, or more commonly with all the baby's usual vaccinations at one month of age.

Week 2-4

By week two the baby hasn't fallen into a predictable routine yet but you are well on the way to forming one. You are knee deep in nursing, rocking and changing nappies, and the baby is becoming more cuddly and alert. You can hear small sounds from your little one and you will notice that the baby seems to intently concentrate on what is going on in their environment. This is called the quiet alert mode.

Mentally, their brain is developing and the proof is in the little sounds they make when awake. Did you know that your baby is learning to focus on your face and memorizing your features in their little brain.

By the fourteenth day after birth, your baby will be back to gaining weight. Around this time, the umbilical cord will fall off and the baby is now feeding every three to four hours.

In the fourth week you probably can't believe how fast time has flown by with your little one in the house. At this time their little hands and legs are constantly flailing as they discover their limbs. Their hearing is now fully developed and they can turn their heads when they hear a sound. Try standing on one side and clicking your fingers. You will notice that they will react and try to turn their head towards you. When it comes to their vision, their sight is becoming stronger; however, you will notice that as they try to focus they may become cross-eyed. If you move an object right before their eyes they will try to follow it. They can focus on an object that is roughly 8-12 inches away.

They are able to try to turn their heads looking for you because their necks are becoming stronger. Now, they can even begin to lift their heads up a bit when they are on their tummy.

Week 5-8

Your baby can smile by week five and is quickly becoming an interactive bundle of dribbles and cuddles. The great news is that having made it through the first month, you are no longer a dazed parent. The baby is still crying but they are also gurgling, cooing and grunting as they discover their tongue and throat and how to make noises. Go ahead and have a conversation with a few of your own coos and grunts. Use some words as well because your baby will soon learn to say mama, dada, baba or whatever simple sounds you teach them at that time. Talk to your baby often, anywhere and about everything. Document your conversation on video or by taking photos which you can enjoy again later or with others.

The baby can sleep for longer at night but wakes up regularly for nursing. They are also still sleeping during the day. You may notice infant acne on their face. These are whiteheads sprinkled all over the skin. They are temporary and will usually clear up naturally in a few weeks.

Between the sixth and eighth week your baby will experience a huge growth spurt. You can expect a smile and recognition of your face when you pass by. They also love brightly coloured items like toys and mobiles.

The baby is learning a lot just spending time interacting with you. You will notice that the baby is following you around with their eyes. They also respond to the sound of your voice by turning to look for you. The head raising is progressing as the baby's neck grows stronger and it is no longer confined to them lying on their tummy. You will also notice it when you hold the baby against your chest. It may seem like the baby is trying to get away from you.

Their limb movements are becoming smoother as they approach their eight-week mark. They are also learning to self soothe by sucking on their fist when distressed. You will notice that they love to look at your face. Peek-a-boo is a fantastic game right now. Babies get bored so you need stimulating activities like a rattle or a colourful ball. At this age babies learn to explore their surroundings by putting what they can into their mouths. This is especially the time to be careful of what small objects are around them!

Going outside is a treat for the baby just as much as it is for you. They are intrigued by the new sounds and sights. Don't be surprised to hear gurgles and coos coming from your stroller as you take a walk. By the eighth week you can begin placing the baby in the baby bouncer at home. Since your infant is now attempting to grab and hold items, make sure you keep unsafe items out of reach.

The good news for you is that around the two-month mark, your baby will begin to have less bowel movements. Until now, they would go after almost every feeding but now they may have only a single bowel movement a day. Breast fed babies can sometimes even go for an entire week with only one bowel movement. This is normal, however, keep an eye out for constipation which may be the cause of not going. Home remedies for constipation include giving the baby a warm bath to relax their muscles and moving their legs gently. You can also give your baby two to four tablespoons of water to help soften their stool. If the constipation persists or occurs frequently you must visit a doctor.

Two-month-olds sleep more at night and stay awake for longer during the day. It is a good time to introduce sleep training by putting them down for a nap when they are drowsy but awake. You can have a signal that the baby associates with sleep like white noise or a lullaby. A gentle infant massage will also do the trick, but don't pull on the arms and legs and don't lean into the baby with any weight.

Week 9-12

This is the third month of life for the new-born. You can see less facial puffiness and more unique features are setting in. Infant features keep changing rapidly as they grow.

At nine weeks your baby is gaining a kilo per week. Aren't you glad you bought that stroller or pram? Otherwise your arms would be exhausted from carrying your lovely bundle around when you are out. Baby's eye and hand coordination has grown as well. For example, they can wiggle their fingers then grab onto something. You will also notice that their eyes follow the movements they make with their hands and that they express delight.

As they move into their tenth week, their legs and hands can make deliberate movements. The movements can be during play or to get something. When they are on their play mat, they will constantly try to raise their head. Don't worry. This is good exercise that strengthens their necks and also tires them out. Parents can begin to massage the baby's little legs and arms after bath time to help with movement and circulation. After having a bath their bodies are more relaxed and the massage will help them sleep soundly.

In their eleventh week, the baby's hearing is more enhanced. This means you can read to the little one. They may respond with a coo as if they understand what you are saying. That's your baby acknowledging the sound of your voice. Invest in a big colourful book to read from in order to stimulate the baby visually as well. When you read, become as animated as you can, and watch their eyes look at you in wonder. Babies also love music at this point, so feel free to sing a lullaby or play calming or cheerful music.

In the final week of the third month the baby is full of adorable expressions. From pouts to serious pensive looks, your baby keeps you guessing about what they are thinking. Maybe they are thinking about you!

They are fascinated by the sound of your voice so have conversations as you do things together. If you don't know what to talk about, explain what you are doing. For example, "It is time for your nap, let's lay you down." or "Let's get you dressed. What do you want to wear today?" These conversations also increase your bond with the baby.

It has been 12 weeks since the baby's arrival, and now they are sleeping for 12 hours a night with only two feeding interruptions. They will still nap around three times during the day but the naps will not be very long. All the developmental milestones you have been seeing in the past few weeks will continue.

How To Care For A 0 to 3-Month-Old Baby

The first few months of life are exciting and daunting for both your baby and you. They don't know where they are, who you are, or understand hunger or a dirty nappy. Everything you do is new to them just as it is for you. Try to understand that they are overwhelmed by their new surroundings. To make the adjustment easier for both you and the baby, follow their lead and diligently meet their physical needs.

Follow Their Lead

Babies will let you know when they are distressed so follow their lead. Do they need to nurse? Feed them. A nappy change? Give them one. Are they sleepy? Put them down to sleep. A baby may not know how to verbalize their needs but they give excellent tips about how they are feeling by crying and making other noises. The good news is that once their need is met your little one will settle down.

Meet Their Physical Needs

Babies need you to meet their physical needs. These are the things that will make them comfortable and allow them to thrive. They need feeding, nappy changes, baths and sleep among other things.

Feeding With Formula

Unless you are breastfeeding your baby you need to learn the best way to mix the baby's formula. Don't worry, it's easy! The formula manufacturer and your lactation specialist at the local hospital will give you the right instructions.

Before you start, there are a few simple guidelines for you to follow.

- Always wash your hands thoroughly before preparing the formula.
- Always check the expiry date on each tin of formula before using it.
- Shake the formula (or powder) container before preparation.
- Use a clean can opener for tinned formula.
- Only use sterile water for the formula preparation.

Preparing Baby Formula

- Measure the advised amount of water into the baby's bottle.
- Scoop the right amount of formula (level scoops) into the bottle with the water.
- Shake the bottle in a hand twist motion for the formula to mix effectively.
- Feed the baby the formula immediately.

It is better to use boiled water that has been cooled instead of bottled water; as bottled water can contain harmful bacteria.

For parents using ready to feed formula all you need to do is to shake the bottle thoroughly before opening it and pour it into the baby's feeding bottle.

Warming Baby Formula

If you have refrigerated baby formula you must bring it to room temperature before feeding it to your baby. Do not warm it in the microwave, convenient as it may be as this can cause uneven heating. Instead, set the baby bottle containing the formula into a large bowl of warm water and let it heat up. You can also hold the bottle under warm tap water.

Lactation experts advise against vigorously shaking the baby formula right before the baby consumes it. The vigorous shaking will cause the formula to get air bubbles that will give your baby gas. This is why it is recommended to use the wrist twisting motion for a thorough mix. However, if you do mix the formula a bit too enthusiastically, don't worry, just set it down for a short while and let the air bubbles settle down before feeding it to the baby.

Reusing Formula

Buying formula is expensive and you may want to save every drop. However, the specific guidelines against saving and reusing formula are important to adhere to. They ensure the safety and wellbeing of your baby. If the baby drinks some formula and doesn't finish it within the hour, discard the remaining formula. Do not warm it or refrigerate it for later reuse. This is because bacteria from the baby's mouth are transferred onto the bottle during feeding. As the bottle of formula is left over, the bacteria continues growing in the bottle. Formula is a perishable product and it can cause food poisoning in your baby. If you notice your baby never finishes the bottle, and you are concerned about wastage, offer a smaller portion.

Storing Formula

Tins of powdered formula can be re-sealed and stored in a cool and dry place. An opened tin should be used within one month (or as described via the instructions on the container). Unused powdered formula should not be stored in the refrigerator. In fact, you should avoid both ends of extreme temperature: too cold or too hot. Freezing will cause the protein and fat in the formula to separate while too much heat will degrade the nutrients.

Ready to feed formula should be stored at room temperature avoiding extreme temperatures as well. The contents in the smaller ready to feed formula bottles can be refrigerated once opened, but they must be used within 24 hours of opening the bottle. Make sure you refrigerate the contents immediately after opening. Never leave the bottle unattended at room temperature and then use the contents later on.

Do's And Don'ts Of Feeding

Feeding should be on demand so take your cues from the baby. From 0-3 months you can expect that the main reason your baby is crying is because they want milk. Plan to feed the baby every two to three hours. Keep tabs on how frequently and how well your baby is feeding. Make sure that your baby has a minimum of 8 feedings in 24 hours.

For breastfeeding mothers, have your nursing chair set up with burp cloths and a blanket to keep you both warm during feeding time. If you are feeding formula, have the essentials to prepare it at hand and ready to use. Imagine having to look for the formula, feeding bottles and water in the middle of the night when the baby is awake and demanding to feed. It is important to think ahead to ensure stress levels are minimal for you both, otherwise that is a recipe for an unhappy parent and unhappy baby!

Feeding is a great time to communicate with your baby. If it is daytime, quietly talk or sing to them or make soothing noises. Not only does it connect you to your little one but it also stimulates their brain.

New parents may fall into the trap of thinking they can anticipate the baby's feeding time and schedule it. However, the little one has plans of their own. During these early months you need to be attentive, alert and prepared for feeding at any time. As a rule, never delay feeding.

If your baby is not breastfeeding, lactation experts advise against giving them whole cow's milk or low fat vegan options like soy or almond milk as an alternative. If you are not breastfeeding, formula is the next best thing for your baby. Some babies have allergic reactions to formula, so be ready to switch brands until you find one that the baby tolerates well. When preparing baby formula make sure you use sterile or boiled water. Also, clean the bottle and nipples thoroughly before each feeding.

Burping

Burping is important for the baby's wellbeing. It removes the air that they swallowed during feeding, which causes them distress. A baby needs to be burped after every meal.

Help the baby to burp by patting their backs gently to aid the air up their oesophagus (or windpipe). The best position to burp a baby is to hold them up to your shoulder facing behind you, lay them face down on your lap or by putting them in a sitting position on your lap. Try all three to find the one that works best for your little one. Keep a cloth on your shoulder or lap to protect your clothing and also have a bib on the baby since they will spit up on themselves. After the baby has burped you can let them feed some more if they want to.

Babies feeding from a bottle should be burped at least once mid-feed to free any air in their stomachs. If the baby is still fussy continue to pat their back to release the air. Breastfeeding babies should be burped when you are switching from one breast to the other. Also try burping them mid-feed to free up the air and then continue with the same breast.

Burping is different from gas although they are both caused by air being trapped in the stomach. Gas is air trapped in the small intestines and it will cause discomfort until the baby passes it out. When babies cry excessively they swallow a lot of air which can also cause gas. Babies also get gas when they are constipated. Their immature digestive system can also trap gas as it strives to process food. This is especially true if you have introduced new food like formula to a breastfed baby.

Gas manifests in babies as a swollen stomach and crying, and the baby will lift their legs and arch their back to find relief. Passing gas is the only way they will find lasting relief.

Changing A Nappy

New-born parents can find nappy changing to be challenging because the baby seems so fragile and it is generally messy and smelly. However, if you handle the baby with care, have the right supplies and learn the basics it will become a very simple task.

Make sure everything you need to change the nappy is at hand. Never leave the baby unattended to fetch an item. At home, it is best to have one spot where you change the baby's nappy and keep everything you need there. In order to develop an easy changing routine, you need to arrange all of your nappy essentials at your baby changing station.

When going out, use your nappy bag to carry your changing pad and other nappy essentials. If you can, have a full extra set in the bag so that you don't have to take anything from your home changing station. This eliminates the chance of forgetting an important item when you are on the go.

How To Change A Nappy?

First, remove the dirty nappy and wipe away the poo using the clean end (the front end) of the nappy. Tuck the dirty nappy up and drop it into the rubbish or nappy bucket.

Using baby wipes, you need to clean the baby's private areas from the front to the back. Gently lift the baby by the ankles enough so that the bottom is off the flat surface. You can also wipe the bottom with a wash cloth dipped in warm water or by using cotton wool. This will clean their bottom completely.

Pat the baby's bottom dry with a towel and apply some barrier lotion or cream to keep their bottom protected. Now place a clean nappy under the baby's bottom and fasten it over the tummy. If you are using a cloth nappy do not forget the inside liner and the waterproof wrap on top. Since babies often urinate or defecate after eating, make it a habit to check the baby's nappy a few times after feeding to make sure you can change them promptly.

Make nappy changing more fun for both baby and parent by singing or making funny faces at your baby to get them giggling happily.

Types Of Baby Stool To Expect

The first stool from your baby will be blackish-green in colour with a sticky consistency. This will come within the first 24 hours after birth. If you are exclusively breastfeeding, the stool will look yellowish and sometimes it may appear pale green. This poo will have a creamy consistency. Formula fed babies will produce pale brown stool which has a pasty almost peanut buttery consistency. It is completely normal to see green stool.

Baths

When the baby is in their first month you can give them a sponge bath. The bath should be in a warm room with a flat surface nearby. Constantly holding the baby up with one hand, gently sponge the baby using warm water and a little body wash. You don't have to lather the little one too much or wash vigorously. If your baby protests against the feeling of water running over their head, you can gently sponge their hair. Rinse them off with warm water and swaddle their body in a towel. When it comes to private parts, wash little girls from the front to the back. For little boys, be very careful with their foreskin, especially if they are circumcised boys and are still healing.

After the bath, dress the baby in warm comfortable clothing to retain their body heat. Socks, a hat, a pair of trousers and a long-sleeved t-shirt are ideal. As they become warmer you should remove layers including their hat and socks.

Skin Care/Baby Eczema

Baby eczema manifests as crusty red patches on the baby's skin and it often occurs within the first few months. Eczema may also present as a series of rashes and small bumps. This type of eczema is known as atopic dermatitis. It appears mostly on the joints of the arms and behind their knees; however, it can appear anywhere on the body including the cheeks.

Eczema is itchy and the skin becomes rough. It can run in families, so if one parent has a tendency to get it, the baby is likely to get it as well. Observe the timing of the rash and try to pinpoint what the cause might be. It can be a reaction to chemicals in shampoos and lotions. Pollen is another big cause of infant eczema as is cow's milk, pets and some types of clothing materials or laundry detergents. For example, some babies are allergic to wool fibres. Having identified the causes, it is easier to keep your baby eczema free.

You can use a humidifier to keep the air in your home moist or bowls of water near a radiator. Dry air can cause your baby to develop eczema since it saps moisture from their skin. Finally, don't give your baby bubble baths. They may be fun for you and the baby, but the overall health implications can be serious. They may cause urinary tract irritation or severe skin irritation and dryness because of the chemicals used in the bubble bath.

Sleep

Babies need sleep to develop and grow. Every new parent learns a vital lesson about baby's sleep when they bring their little one home. There is more to getting them to sleep than just rocking them. For the first two months you need to hold your baby and soothe them to sleep. By the third month your baby will nod off on their own.

Dress the baby in light sleep clothes and regulate the temperature in the room to prevent overheating which can contribute to incidences of Sudden Infant Death Syndrome (SIDS). Use lighting in the baby's room strategically. Place the lights in corners where they will illuminate the room without being too bright or over the baby cot. Using a dark lampshade or a light dimmer will provide a cosy ambiance for breastfeeding.

Things To Avoid At Sleep Time

During night feeds try not to look directly into the baby's eyes because eye contact is an invitation for the baby to interact with you. You want them to slide back into sleep after feeding, not to become stimulated and intrigued by your face. This is also true of the sound of your voice so don't talk unless you absolutely have to and even then keep a low voice. The night feed is known as the dream feed because the baby is oscillating between sleep and wakefulness. Tip the scales in favour of sleep by keeping your face as unanimated as possible.

Don't place your baby on their tummy to sleep. This sleeping position increases the chances of cot death, commonly known as SIDS. The safest sleeping position for a baby in this age group is on their back. Sleeping on their back allows them to breathe easily and without any restrictive materials near their nose.

It is also important to keep the baby's crib clutter free in order to prevent the baby from suffocating. Do not leave stuffed animals or other toys in their crib as they sleep. Also, keep blankets and pillows out of this space. Babies do not need to be covered with quilts and blankets. Don't rush sleep training in the first few weeks. Sleep training is not important for a baby at this time as they sleep most of the time.

Safe Travel

Invest in a stroller or pram that has an expandable canopy. This protects the baby from too much sun and also moderates the amount of stimulation they are exposed to. Babies love to sleep during their outdoor excursions in the stroller. Fresh air and the gentle rocking motion of the stroller or pram is soothing to them.

Buy a baby carrier that is a front mounting unit with straps that fit comfortably for both you and the baby. Buy one that will fit their bodies even as they grow in the coming weeks. Also, make sure that the straps are adjustable for you and can accommodate any weight gain or loss you experience. The carrier should be lightweight and made of a wicking fabric.

Choose baby friendly destinations when traveling with the baby. These are places with changing areas and breastfeeding sections where you can comfortably take care of the baby. Always pack the essentials you need for nursing, nappy changes and first aid.

When installing and using a car seat, do not deviate from the manufacturer's instructions on how to use it. Rear facing seats must not be used as forward-facing seats and vice versa. A car seat is precisely designed in order to properly mount onto the seat in the vehicle. Furthermore, they are meant to be used only in the rear seat of your car.

Safe Handling

When handling a baby, hygiene is paramount. Anyone handling the new-born needs to wash their hands thoroughly. Some parents even insist on a change of clothes when you enter the house before touching the baby. This may seem a bit excessive to some people but others feel the need to implement extra safety measures to safeguard the baby. For example, if your partner works with chemicals it would make sense for them to shower and change if possible before handling the baby. It is also okay to use hand sanitiser as well instead of hand washing all the time, but don't use it on the baby.

Support the baby's neck and head every time you handle the baby. Cradle the head when you are carrying your baby upright and when laying them down because their skull is very delicate. The baby's neck is also very fragile during this time so handle them with utmost care. If you don't take care to handle these areas carefully you will leave the baby vulnerable to brain injury.

Never shake the baby out of frustration or when waking them up. Shaking causes bleeding in the baby's brain and sometimes leads to death. Rough play can also be dangerous so play very gently with the baby. Innocent games like bouncing the baby on the knee or throwing them in the air can be too vigorous. Some parents like to exercise with their babies but rigorous exercise while carrying the baby can hurt them when they are very young.

Swaddling is a common practice but don't smother the baby in the swaddling clothes. Do not swaddle your baby all the time because this limits the baby's reflex and growth. When the baby is at home with you there is no need to keep them swaddled. When your baby is unswaddled you have more opportunities for skin to skin contact.

Common Challenges With A 0 To 3-Month-Old Baby

Latching

Latching is the act of the baby engaging with mum's breast to begin breastfeeding. The secret to latching is helping your baby to close their mouth around the areola (the dark covering on the skin that surrounds the nipple). If the baby latches onto the nipple only, your nipples will become sore and crack. Milk comes from little openings in the nipple which release the milk once the areola is pressed. That is why the baby's mouth needs to encompass part of the areola. Babies are not born knowing exactly how to latch on. This is a learned habit and you can help the baby along.

To help the baby latch on you need to hold them in the right breastfeeding position. Hold your breast in your free hand. Your thumb should be above your nipple and the index finger below the nipple. Use the two fingers to demarcate where your baby's nose and chin will rest on the breast during nursing. Now press the breast to jut it out and protrude it towards the baby's mouth.

To help your baby latch, stimulate the rooting reflex of the baby by stroking the baby's cheek. The baby's first attempt will most probably result in latching onto the nipple. You will hear clicking sounds and feel pain in your nipple as your baby chews on it in an attempt to latch on. Unlatch and guide the little mouth back to the larger area of the areola and nipple.

Poor latching can be a result of poor positioning. There are five breastfeeding positions that will help you get the baby to latch on.

Crossover: In this position the baby lies in the crook of your arm resting their tummy on yours. You should support the head and turn the baby towards you allowing their mouth to align to the breast.

Cradle hold: This position entails cradling the baby with your forearm. Their head rests on the forearm on the same side with the breast you are using to breastfeed.

Football hold: With this position, your baby's legs are tucked under your arm on the same side as the breast you are using. This is a great option if you have had a c-section, have a premature baby or have twins. You can use a breastfeeding pillow in this position for comfort.

Side lying: You can breastfeed the baby without having to leave the bed. This is more common if you are co-sleeping with your baby. Many experts caution against co-sleeping due to the higher risk of smothering the baby by accident. Lay your baby tummy to tummy with you and guide the breast into the baby's mouth. If you are using this position, ensure that you do not fall asleep with the baby on the breast.

Laid back: If you have smaller breasts, this may be a more comfortable position for you. Lean back in the chair and allow the baby to reach your breast from any direction. Leaning back and gravity both help the baby to reach your areola easily.

Poor latching can also be a result of holding the baby too far away or hunching over the baby and pushing the breast into their mouth instead of bringing the baby to you. Another reason can be if you have inverted or flat nipples which makes it harder for the baby to latch on. Try and hold the breast while pulling the tissue around the nipple back so that the nipple is exposed and can fit into the baby's mouth. Alternatively seek professional help from your midwife if you're encountering problems, there is a lot of support if needed. If all this fails then consider a breast pump to express the milk.

Crying

Crying is how a new-born communicates displeasure. Their displeasure is mainly as a result of discomfort. This sound has an electrifying effect on parents that spurs them into action. For mums it triggers the let-down reflex. This is the reflex that causes your breast milk to be produced. Your little one will cry the most for the next six weeks. Infants cry for a myriad of reasons including a full nappy, hunger and sleepiness. It is quite natural and okay to pick up your baby as soon as they begin to cry. Responding quickly prevents the baby's distress from escalating. Picking up your little one makes them feel safe and loved. Sometimes all they need is a cuddle to calm them down.

Colic is a cause of incessant crying in new-borns and colicky babies can be challenging to sooth. It is believed to be caused by a reaction to foods in mum's diet, or as an allergy to cow's milk proteins in formula. To soothe a colicky baby:

- Reduce stimulation by sitting with the baby in a dimmed room

- Lay the baby on their side and pat their back rhythmically. If they fall asleep turn them gently on their back.
- Take a walk with the baby. It is preferable to use a sling rather than the pram so that they are snuggled into you.
- Gripe water is recommended for young babies. Make sure the instructions are followed and give only the recommended dosage.
- Use a white noise machine to soothe the baby.
- Evaluate the diet of both baby and mum and determine if there are any foods that should be eliminated.

Babies use five distinct types of cries to communicate how they are feeling. Here is how to decode your baby's communication:

"Neh": This type of cry tells you that your baby is hungry. The "n" in the cry comes about because the baby is touching their tongue to the roof of the mouth due to the sucking reflex. It is usually preceded by the baby making sucking sounds.

"Eair": When your baby is uncomfortable from gas or from not having burped properly they will tend to cry with a sigh. This is their way of trying to push the gas out of their stomachs. At the same time the baby will pull their legs towards their stomach.

"Heh": Heh signifies any other type of discomfort from a wet nappy to an uncomfortable nappy rash. This cry can be confused for the hunger cry.

"Eh": This cry has a short, staccato sound signalling that the baby is in pain or feeling unwell. It can mean that the baby is in physical distress from a fever or an infection that is causing them pain. Check their temperature using the baby thermometer and take them to the paediatrician.

"Owh": The "owh" cry signifies that the baby is getting drowsy and sleepy. The sound is close to a yawn indicating that the baby is tired. It is often accompanied by rubbing the eyes and actual yawns.

Things To Look Out For With A 0 To 3-Month-Old Baby

Choking

Choking in infants is caused by a blockage to their air passageways. In the case of new-borns it can be from ingesting too much milk. Three-month-olds have some hand-mouth coordination so they can put a small object like a button or part of a toy into their mouth. If choking occurs, give your baby five moderately hard back slaps as they lay across your thighs with their head dipped down. Hit them firmly in the space between their shoulder blades. The back slaps cause a vibration that dislodges the item, but it is important to support their head as you administer the slaps and not to hit too hard.

If the situation becomes serious, call the emergency lines and get medics on the way to come and help you. Even if you are able to dislodge the item that caused the choking, your baby will need a check up to ensure they are okay. In case you can't dislodge the item, medical help will be on their way.

Chest thrusts, also known as chest compressions, can also be effective. Turn the baby to face upwards and push downwards in the middle of their chest right below the nipples. This can sharply push the air out of their lungs and dislodge the item. Again, be careful, as you can really hurt them.

Difficulty Breathing

The main sign that your baby is having breathing difficulty is an increase in the breathing rate of the baby (more than 60 breaths per minute). You may also notice that the baby is grunting at the end of every breath and their nostrils are flaring as the baby tries to suck in more air. The baby's chest falls and expands more than normal. You will also see the baby's lips and tongue turn blue as the oxygen levels in their blood falls.

If you notice your baby is having difficulty breathing, go to the emergency room immediately.

Cot Death

As we have previously mentioned, cot death is another reference to Sudden Infant Death Syndrome (SIDS). This is the sudden and unexplained death of a healthy baby usually during sleep. It occurs with a higher prevalence in premature babies or in infants with a low birth weight, occurs more in boys than girls and it happens within the first six months. The good news is that cot death is not common and the risk of losing your baby to it is very low if you practice safe sleep habits. Most importantly, babies should always sleep on their back, not their stomach. Regulating the temperature in the baby's room is also crucial, ideally the temperature should be between 16-20 degrees Celsius. It prevents the baby from being too hot or too cold. Allow them to sleep in the same room with you for the first six months so that you can monitor their sleep.

Common Questions About 0 To 3-Month-Old Babies

Should I take a first aid course before my new-born arrives?

Some day you may have to save your baby's life or treat them for a wound before you can get them to a hospital. A baby first aid course is crucial because it equips you with basic and simple skills for handling everyday situations that could turn tragic. The basic course will teach you how to deal with your baby choking, sustaining a burn, experiencing a seizure or high fever. You will also learn what to do when your baby bumps their head or if they swallow something harmful.

Why is tummy time important?

Tummy time is the time the baby spends on their stomach. This allows them to develop and strengthen their neck, shoulder, stomach and back muscles. The baby will try to raise their head and turn it around. At first, make sure you always support their head and make sure they don't place their face down and suffocate. Soon you will not need to support their head because their muscles will become strong enough to do it. Paediatricians recommend starting regular tummy time soon after you bring your baby home. Start with a few minutes every day. By three months old your baby should be getting an hour of tummy time a day.

This exercise sets them up for crawling, sitting and rolling in later months. It also helps to prevent delays in early motor milestones and aids in body awareness. You can use the tummy time techniques below:

- **Tummy to tummy/chest:** Place your baby on your tummy face down on their tummy.
- **Tummy down carry:** Carry the baby on their tummy. Place your hand between the baby's legs and hold their tummy while carrying them. Gently support their head.
- **Eye level smile:** Place the baby on their tummy and lie on your tummy opposite them and encourage eye contact.
- **Tummy minute:** Let the baby spend a minute or two on their tummy on a flat surface after every nappy change.

Can I use formula and breastfeed as well?

Yes, you can. This method of nursing the baby is known as supplementing. It is safe and okay to use this method especially if you have to go back to work. Many families adopt this method either out of preference, convenience or necessity.

Introduce formula to your baby gradually if possible. Let your baby breastfeed and supplement their milk in the next feeding session. Mixed feeding gives you the best of both worlds. If you start supplementing with formula, keep an eye out for allergic reactions.

Chapter Four: Four to Six Months

"Babies should be classified as an antidepressant. It's pretty hard to be in a bad mood around a 5-month old baby." – Jim Gaffigan

Your baby is almost at the halfway mark of their first year. Your baby is changing and growing so fast that sometimes you feel like if you blink you might miss something. Don't worry, you have plenty of time to enjoy the baby as they grow.

Developmental Expectations

Fourth Month

At this age the baby is beginning to see their world in full colour. In the past weeks your baby would react to your photograph with the same level of interest as they would with you in person. By the fourteenth week, they are able to discern the real you from an image of you because your colours are more pronounced. Here is a little colour test: leave a bright red, yellow, green or blue toy in front of your baby as well as a brown one. Your little one will choose the brighter coloured toy over the dull one.

Around the sixteenth week your baby's eye colour is starting to change from what they had from birth. If the eyes were dark coloured such as deep brown they will maintain the same hue but light coloured eyes may darken. For example, if the eyes were caramel in colour they will become brown and paler eyes may settle into green or blue. In a few weeks the eye colour will become permanent.

During this time, you may also notice that sometimes your baby is cross-eyed. This eye immaturity is normal at this stage of your baby's growth. Eye immaturity is different from a lazy eye which doctors might check for around this age. Lazy eye (or cross-eye) is medically known as amblyopia and it reduces vision in one eye as that eye turns outwards or inwards. This condition develops in children between birth and their seventh birthday. Fortunately, a lazy eye can be treated as long as you catch it early and get medical attention.

Within the fourth month your baby is honing their motor activities further by learning to roll over and clapping. There is also lots of laughing. There is no hard timeline for these milestones though so you may notice them even more in your baby as they progress into the fifth and sixth months.

Fifth Month

In the fifth month you can expect to see your baby sitting more and for longer periods of time. Of course, you still need to prop them up with a pillow but in time they are able to sit unsupported for a few seconds. Your baby may also be able to rollover from their back to their tummy. They also begin to work their legs during tummy time in preparation for their six and seven month milestone of crawling. Since your baby can roll, make sure you do not leave them unattended at any time on a surface where they can fall over.

As your baby grows and becomes stronger, expect your little one's grasp to be firmer. They can hang onto an item in their hand for longer and move it from one hand to another. They may even hold on to their feeding bottle on their own.

It's been five months of interrupted sleep and now your baby may be able to sleep through the night, but don't be discouraged if they don't. Encourage your baby to get into a sleep rhythm by establishing a bedtime routine. A simple night time routine is the key to proper sleep training. Start with a warm bath, feed the baby if they need it, and hold them until they become drowsy. When the baby's eyes begin to droop, place them in their cot and let them drift off on their own.

During the day your five-month-old will require two naps which will probably occur mid-morning and early to mid-afternoon. Do not delay the baby's naps otherwise they won't sleep properly during the night.

The baby's vision has improved further into their fifth month. Babies still don't have 20/20 vision by this time but they begin to focus more clearly on items without becoming cross-eyed. They can also differentiate between two shades of one colour.

Their vision is not the only thing that is becoming better. Your baby is beginning to babble. All those days of talking to your baby are beginning to pay off. So don't stop now. Keep talking to your little one and they will soon learn how to put vowels and consonants together. That is when you will hear the precious first words ma-ma, da-da, ba-ba or other recognition words you have been waiting for. The baby hasn't yet assigned meaning to the sounds escaping their mouth. In a couple of months, they will associate words like ma-ma with you because you will reinforce it.

However, your baby is now able to identify different words and sounds. For example, they can make sense of a dog barking or a car honking. Most importantly, when you say the word "no" your little one can make sense of the command. This month, invest in playing with your baby using colourful toys and say the name of each toy out loud. This will help teach your baby new words and also help them identify their toys. Also, play music more often for the baby so they can hear some more new words. They may not be able to sing but they will enjoy hearing words flowing in music.

Sixth Month

Your baby is becoming a more independent tiny human and they have doubled their birth weight. After this month their weight gain will begin to slow down to about half a kilogram per month. Their height growth will also slow down to a few centimetres per month in the subsequent months. Your baby's motor skills have grown tremendously. They can sit up on their own by propping themselves up with their hands and they will also move around the floor by rolling around or creeping backwards and forwards. In addition, they are also pushing up against the floor with their hands and sometimes they rise up on their knees and arms. When they get on their hands and knees they may rock back and forth. Look out for the baby also rolling from their back to their tummy and then back again.

Sleep is progressively becoming a six to eight hours affair for the baby, but they may still wake up sometimes in the night. Since they can roll from their back to their stomachs you may notice that you put them to sleep on their back but they wake up on their stomach. The risk of cot death reduces significantly by this age so if the baby is sleeping on their tummy they are safe. However, continue to keep stuffed toys, blankets and pillows out of the cot while the baby is sleeping. The silver lining here is that since your baby is sleeping for longer stretches at night, you can go back to having longer periods of sleep yourself.

You will also be able to start feeding your baby on some solid food like pureed fruits and some soft iron-fortified cereal. Introduce new foods one at a time giving the baby a few days to get accustomed to the food and see if there is any allergic reaction. If you have any concerns don't be afraid to visit your local paediatrician to discuss the best foods for your baby at this time.

Some great food choices for your baby include:

- Bananas
- Avocado
- Shredded fish
- Pureed beans
- Cheese and yogurt
- Pureed broccoli, spinach and kale
- Water with fluoride
- Carrots and celery sticks

Don't give up on a food if your baby rejects it the first time. Give it to them again after a few days to see if the reaction is the same. Do this until your baby is used to the foods. This is a time of trial and error so be patient with yourself and your baby too. If you notice your baby gets a rash, begins vomiting or gets diarrhoea, stop offering that food until the baby is older and then try again.

Your baby is becoming quite vocal in their sixth month. Reading to them will help them learn the language and soon they will have a few almost recognizable words to say. The baby is also starting to get familiar with the people who surround them. For example, they recognize you, your partner and other members of the close family or support system. When with strangers they will probably cry or become fussy.

Encouraging Baby Communication

Watch

Look at your baby and see what they are doing with their hands. When your little one wants you to pick them up they will raise their arms towards you. If they reach for a toy then they may want to play. If they play with their food they may be signalling that they have had enough to eat.

As you respond to your baby you can verbalize certain words that communicate what the baby is feeling. For example, if the baby pushes the plate away ask them, "full now?" If they reach for a toy then say the word, "play." When they lift their arms to you ask, "carry you?" Soon they will associate these words with their actions and eventually learn to say them when they want something specific.

Narrate

Babies love to listen to the sound of your voice but since they also pick up on words that you say, use appropriate language. Reading to them or narrating what you are doing is a great way to help them grasp the language. When you are getting a snack for them you can say, "I am making your snack. Do you want to eat some yummy peaches?"

Praise

Positive reinforcement helps your baby to know good actions versus bad actions. They also learn what makes you happy. Your baby loves your smile and happy words so when they finish their food smile at them and praise them while giving them a cuddle. Soon they will learn to smile when they are happy about something.

Imitate

Babies are great at imitating you. In fact, this is how they learn. They also have fun when you imitate them. When they say ma-ma or da-da or other words you should say it back to them. Soon when you say, "I love you" they will try to do the same. They may not get it right but they are definitely learning. When they see you playing with a toy, they will try to imitate you.

Exercises To Strengthen The Baby's Tummy

Baby Cobra

Let your baby lie on their tummy and play with a rattle slightly above their head. They will attempt to rise on their hands to get a better view of the rattle. Make sure the rattle is not too far above their heads. They should be able to see it even while lying down.

Twist And Roll

Since your baby is able to roll from their back to their tummy and vice versa, place a rattle (or their favourite toy) slightly out of reach so that they have to roll or twist towards it. When they begin to twist towards it their body will automatically roll over as well.

Sit Up

This activity entails helping your baby use their stomach muscles to stay upright. Sit them on a soft surface like the sofa and sit at their feet. Hold your baby's hands to offer support but try not to prop them up. Do not let the baby struggle because that may be frustrating for them. With time their stomach muscles will strengthen and they will be able to sit on their own.

Teething

At this age, your baby's milk teeth are usually growing in and this is uncomfortable for them. The first teeth to come in are usually the lower front teeth (the lower incisors).

As the first few emerge there will be a lot of drooling and fussiness. To make the teething period manageable you can help soothe the baby's gums by giving them a cold washcloth to chew on. Some parents buy chew toys for their little ones but be careful to buy products that are safe and designed for baby use. Topical pain relievers are not recommended for the teething process because they may contain chemicals like benzocaine which can have dangerous side effects such as trouble breathing, a racing heartbeat and headache. If your baby is very uncomfortable, your doctor can prescribe a weight appropriate dose of oral pain reliever to help manage the pain.

As the teeth come in it is important to begin good oral hygiene habits. Fluoride helps prevent tooth decay by hardening the tooth enamel. Small sips of water containing fluoride will help strengthen your baby's teeth. Brush their teeth with a soft bristled toothbrush with a tiny smear of fluoride toothpaste about the size of a grain of rice. Brush the teeth (even if it is one) twice a day with the last brushing after their last meal. Do not put a bottle into the cot with them and let them feed while they fall asleep. This can result in tooth decay because your baby's teeth are not clean while they sleep. Giving your baby water with fluoride and brushing their teeth with fluoride toothpaste is usually enough to keep their teeth healthy.

Common Questions About 3 To 6-Month-Old Babies

Can I stop worrying about cot death yet?

Doctors believe that once the baby is about six months old, and they are able to lift their head and roll from back to tummy they are in less danger of cot death. As long as parents do not clutter the baby's cot with stuffed animals or blankets, your baby will breathe easily and stay safe from suffocation after the sixth month mark.

Why is my 4-month-old baby fussy suddenly?

Apart from needing a nappy change and being hungry, your baby can often become fussy when experiencing a growth spurt. The fourth month comes with many growth developments and your baby may also feel overstimulated sometimes. This may cause them to become over tired and fussy. Develop a few strategies to help them calm down. To begin with, reduce stimulation by going with the baby into a dim room. Turn on a white noise machine or dishwasher in the other room, rock the baby or nurse them while you move around slowly.

Remember that your baby is getting used to their new environment and every day they can do something new. It is okay for them to be overwhelmed sometimes and they will get past this fussy phase.

Chapter Five: Seven to Nine Months

"It is way too early for him to be talking anyhow but I see in his eyes something and I see in his eyes a voice and I see in his eyes a whole new set of words." - Sherman Alexie

Indeed, your little one has so much to say and they are saying it through their eyes, actions and gurgles. As Sherman suggests here, your baby's personality is now beginning to slowly emerge and you can witness this through their interaction with the world.

Developmental Expectations

Seventh Month

At this age your baby is becoming more mobile and will move around in a combination of movements including scooting, crawling and rolling. Their movements are becoming more controlled and they are becoming curious little explorers.

Parents are able to get more done during the day now since the baby can sit on their own and they can reach out for their toys unaided. Do you know that your baby can now stand on their feet if you hold them up? Holding them up for a few minutes will help strengthen their leg muscles which will help them to begin walking. Also, your little one can hold a spoon and cup and attempt to eat from their plate at meal times.

At seven months your baby is eating chunkier solid foods like potatoes and some vegetables. Moving your baby from pureed food to semi solid food is crucial at this time because it helps them adapt to chewing regular food. Iron fortified cereals, pulses and beans as well as oatmeal and eggs should be a staple for your 7-month-old. These foods are essential in strengthening bones and teeth.

Laughter, chuckling, gurgles and babbling are the main communication tools for the baby. Expect separation and stranger anxiety during this time. Stranger anxiety is when your infant gets upset around people they don't know. This may keep occurring until your little one grows older. Separation anxiety is also called separation protest and it begins in infants around seven months old. It will likely peak at one and a half years. It is normal for your baby to feel this way because these behaviours are part of their survival instinct. They recognise that their wellbeing is tied to yours because they trust you. They don't have the same level of trust for strangers and being separated from you leaves them vulnerable.

Eighth Month

Your baby is now considered an infant. They are eating three balanced meals a day and a snack in between. It is crucial to make sure the baby is having their breakfast, lunch and dinner. The portions don't have to be large otherwise the baby will not finish the food. Four to six tablespoons will suffice for each meal and this portion size can be sustained through into the ninth month. It may seem like a small portion but for a baby it is quite adequate. You can offer snacks like a piece of mango in between meals.

Infants are sleeping an average of thirteen to fourteen hours a day. This includes sleeping through much of the night and taking two naps during the day. An interesting development during this month is seeing your baby bounce on their feet when standing. This means that the baby is able to bear more weight on their legs. Your baby is also able to pull themselves upright using furniture for support.

By the eighth month, your baby is learning fast. For example, they can now learn new words so introduce more music like lullabies, read to the baby more and make some conversation. Although they won't burst into song or give you an earful about how their day was, their brains are learning the sounds you make and memorizing them for the future. When you talk to your baby, they will respond with sounds like eh, ah, mm, baa, and oh among others.

When your little one is frustrated they will have corresponding emotions and sounds. You will also notice your baby will respond to your emotions and tone of voice. When you speak sharply to them they will probably begin to cry and when you smile they will smile back at you. In their eighth month the baby will have less nursing sessions but they still need to be breastfed or continue drinking formula.

You can also take your little one outdoors more to further stimulate their brains. The baby's eyesight is almost as good as an adult's now so they can really take in the sights around them. When you take them out, make sure you apply some baby friendly sunscreen on them to prevent sunburn.

Ninth Month

Your baby is crawling and is even waving bye when you leave the house. They are also experimenting with the textures of new foods that you are introducing. They are showing traits like determination and stubbornness. At this time, parents should begin instilling some discipline by teaching them to obey the words "no" and "stop." Learning these words can keep them from harm. The best way to discipline a child of this age is to be consistent about what you say no to. For example, if you don't like it when the baby pulls your hair while breastfeeding, you must consistently tell them "no" in a firm tone while removing their hand. Soon they will understand that this is not acceptable behaviour.

As the baby continues learning to walk they will start to lose some of their chubbiness and gain more muscle. Your little one is almost a toddler now and they are beginning to act like one. They are waddling around on their chubby legs and slowly moving from crawling to walking. You will also notice that your baby is grabbing for the items they want so make sure hazardous items are stored away.

It is okay to keep breastfeeding; however, make sure the baby eats their solid food at meal time and breastfeed them after. You can also start to introduce a sip of water after their meal. Your baby can get distracted when nursing and they may begin to play or turn their head with your nipple in the mouth. They may even bite down on your nipple. Remind them that this is unacceptable with another firm "no" and take your nipple from their mouth.

Sleep patterns are still similar to the seventh month. The baby is sleeping through the night with maybe a nap or two during the day. The baby gets tired playing all throughout the day. Make sure they always go to bed early to ensure they get adequate rest. It is important to have an established night time routine to signal to the baby that it is time to sleep. For example, get them to say goodnight to everyone in the living room, settle down in the baby's room and read a bedtime story. If you make this a nightly ritual your baby will learn that these cues mean it is time to sleep.

A Healthy Balanced Diet

At this age your baby is able to eat foods from all the food groups: carbohydrates, proteins, dairy, vegetables and fruit. Your baby will easily eat carbohydrates like soft breads, rice and soft noodles. Another food they will easily eat is dairy products. They are already used to breastmilk or formula so they adapt easily to products containing dairy. When introducing dairy products and any other new food, watch for allergic reactions. Children are sometimes allergic to cow's milk or nuts, among other foods.

They don't yet have the teeth to chew on meat, but they will eat chicken that has been softened or shredded. Soften meat products by shredding or pureeing and mixing them with other foods to make it easier for the baby to eat and digest. Let your baby give you cues when it comes to feeding. Since they will eat when they are hungry, usually infants don't have any food hang ups and will gobble up most offerings. Their stomachs are small so a few tablespoons are quite sufficient to satisfy them. New parents may feel that they always have to prepare a special meal for the baby, but this is not true! It is okay to feed your baby the same thing you are eating, as long as it is simple food that is nutritious, not spicy and made into pieces that are easy enough for them to eat.

Encouraging A 9-Month-Old To Talk

Give your baby the opportunity to babble to you and respond back. Look them in the eye and talk to them in a conversational tone. Keep an eye on their non-verbal communication, such as watching their hands to see what they are pointing at.

At nine months-old you need to be careful how you communicate to your baby. They are learning so much from you and they will try to imitate you. Consider the following:

Pitch and Tone

Your pitch and tone are important and communicate different things to the baby. Speaking softly in a near whisper means that it is time to sleep, whereas being loud will convey excitement and activity, which will in turn excite your child. They can tell when you are happy or upset from the pitch and tone of your voice.

Babies also respond to inflection so try to put inflections in your words. For example, if you are going out you can ask them, "Do you want to go out?" The upward inflection should be on the last word "out". New parents will also find that they can captivate their babies by talking in different funny voices. This is because babies love the interesting pitches and tones. During story time try being a gruffy bear one minute and a squeaky mouse the next.

Follow Their Lead

When your baby is curious about something they will show interest in it, sometimes by pointing at it. Take the opportunity to point at it, pick it up if possible and explain what it is. This is more likely to happen when there is new stimuli around and when they are outdoors.

Singing

Singing is one of the most interactive ways of communicating with your baby. During a bath you can sing a song for the parts of their body that you are washing. Nursery rhymes are excellent for teaching your baby new words. Some old nursery rhymes like Old MacDonald's Farm work just as well today as they did when you were a baby.

Piggyback Words

As the baby grows they will start to respond better to two word sentences. Introduce them to piggyback words like "sleepy time", "play time", "drink juice" and "snack time". They will learn them from hearing you and say them when they really begin to talk. Make a point of talking to your baby throughout the day and make sure you are also using real sentences like "Do you want to eat?" and "It is playtime?" and "How about some yogurt." The constant exposure to the language will help them learn to speak properly.

Common Questions About 7 To 9-Month-Old Babies

What should I expect at the 9-month baby wellness check-up?

The nine-month wellness check-up will inform you about the baby's development in terms of motor skills and communication. The doctor will also check up on your little one's nutrition and ask you about their sleep patterns. The baby will also be given any vaccinations they need. You can expect questions about your baby's mobility, such as: "Are they sitting by themselves?" or "Are they waving to you?" and "Do they respond to their name or a loud command?"

What are the best foods for a 9-month-old baby?

Your baby is able to eat the same types of foods that you typically stock up in your pantry and fridge. Remember, it is about ease and safety. Small pieces of bland food are best. It can be helpful to pre-plan their meals in advance. Here is a quick sample that you can use as a guide:

Breakfast

- Oatmeal
- Pancakes
- Waffles
- Eggs scrambled or as an omelette

Lunch

- Bread with crust cut off and some avocado slices or soft cheese
- Unsweetened yogurt with chunks of soft or steamed fruit
- Soup with soft vegetables
- Macaroni and cheese with pureed vegetables

Dinner

- A baked sweet potato
- Rice or pasta with a light sauce that includes some soft vegetables
- Noodles with some soft vegetables

Snacks

- Start with some pureed fruits and gradually introduce small chunks of soft fruit
- Give the baby a small slice of cheese to snack on
- Avoid biscuits because the small bits that break off from the biscuits can become a choking hazard

Chapter Six: Ten to Twelve Months

*"You'd be surprised how durable babies are. You hold
them like Fabergé eggs and then – wonk! - she hits her
head on the table and you think 'oh my gosh, did I give her
a dent on her head that's going to be there forever?' But
babies aren't that precious. Everyone turns out just fine.
Just love them and make them laugh. I make my daughter
laugh every day."* – Jimmy Fallon.

Babies are stronger than we think and by the tenth
month, they are becoming more independent by the day.
Your child will fall and get scrapes and there will be many
tearful moments. The best remedy is to not overreact and
soothe them with emotional comfort. Where possible laugh
with them in an encouraging tone. Get used to it because at
this age there will be many falls and scrapes. It is important
to set a good tone for how your child reacts and what they
need from you. Your little one will be okay! Enjoy their
every show of independence and keep your first aid kit
around to treat cuts and scrapes.

Developmental Expectations

Tenth Month

This month you are beginning to get a sense of your
baby's personality. They are unique little people now and
have identified their favourite items like a book, toy, song
and stuffed animal. They will probably become attached to
certain items and want them around to soothe them. For

example, a favourite blanket will help them settle down or a fun toy will make them want to play.

Your 10-month-old has become excellent at crawling and can stand and sit back down on their own. You will find them cruising around using furniture to support themselves. They are more coordinated now which helps them to move around faster. If your house isn't baby proofed by now, you need to take care of that to ensure their safety.

There are several things you can do to baby proof your home. Acquire a play pen to confine your baby in their play space. Install a gate at the top and bottom of the staircase to prevent them from playing on the stairway unsupervised. You should also invest in electric outlet plug covers, window guards, bumpers for the corners of furniture and latches for all drawers or cupboards they can reach. On cabinets you can use sliding locks, Velcro or cover the knobs to prevent them from pulling them open.

A 10-month-old loves to stack items up into a skyscraper and then watch them tumble down. Invest in stack toys which will help with their coordination. At this age they can hold one item in one hand and use their other hand on another task.

You will notice that your baby takes only a single nap a day now, and they are sleeping adequately through the night. It is okay if they are still taking two naps a day. For those taking single naps, it is best to let them nap in the early afternoon to avoid pre-bedtime crankiness.

A few more teeth are coming in now so your little one is able to chew more and eat foods with thicker consistencies. They may want to feed themselves using a spoon or by picking up the food and putting it in their mouth. Expect a mess when they eat. This is all part of the process of refining their hand to mouth coordination.

At this age your baby is likely to mimic what you do. To your baby you are a prime influencer, and they will try to simulate and repeat any actions you make in front of them. If you are combing your hair they will try to do the same. They also recognize your car, the family pet and their caregivers. They will try to respond to you.

Eleventh Month

Your baby continues on their growth trajectory and is developing stronger leg muscles that can now allow him or her to take a few steps on their own. Their first birthday is fast approaching so prepare to mark their first complete year in your lives.

They now have better balance while standing, so you may notice them standing on their toes to reach for something on the counter. Adventurous little ones will develop a love for climbing and they may try to climb over the cot railing and other baby proofed areas of the house. Prevent dangerous situations without curtailing your baby's adventurous nature. For example, move chairs away from the counter, install the TV on the wall and hide electric cables. Some parents create a safe route for the baby to play and move along. This is a great way to encourage the baby to explore while keeping them safe.

They are still happy to stack up blocks so let them continue playing this game until they become bored. Their taste buds are also evolving so it is a good time to introduce them to new flavours. Do not force your baby to finish their food. Let them push away their dish when they are full.

Your baby can now probably say the word "no". They are also learning to throw a tantrum and can see how you react to it. When you name something familiar to them they can point it out. For example, if you say the dog's name they will point to it. They can also respond to you when you ask them a question. It may not be a proper response but it is an acknowledgment of your words. For example, if you say, "Do you want to play?", they may respond with "babababa" followed by pointing to a toy and squealing. It may not be a coherent response, but it is a response nonetheless!

Twelfth Month

Congratulations, your baby is nearing the end of their first year! They are now feeding themselves more effectively and their playtime is more interactive.

Your baby is probably walking on their own, cooperates more when it's time to get dressed and can follow simple instructions. Parenting a 12-month-old can be quite exhausting, so make sure you get help from your support network if you have one. Call someone to relieve you for a few hours, then go and do something relaxing for yourself. When you come back you will be more rested and able to enjoy the baby without feeling run down.

Activities To Boost A 9 To 12-Month-Old's Development

Use A Toy Storage Box

This box or basket is where toys are generally kept. Help your baby place their toys in the box and help them remove them. Use words like "get toy" and "put back toy". Make this a game to encourage fine motor skills like grasping items and coordination skills like putting the items back. Make sure the basket or box is not too deep and is placed on a flat stable surface. Only use the box for the baby's items so they know this is a place that is always a safe source of their own toys. When you are tidying their toys, talk to them and get them to help.

Toys To Help Develop The Five Senses

Sound

Sound is a wonderful way to engage the baby's imagination. Using toys that react with sound when touched by the baby, such as a toy drum, toy piano, or soft squeaky toy can really aid development. There are also sound activated fun pads that make sounds when the keys are pressed. Some even have pictures of animals and when you press the button it says what animal it is and makes that animal sound!

Touch

Teething toys can also be touch toys. They allow your baby to explore a different texture in their mouth. Common toys like rattles and little stuffed animals can also work well as touch toys because your baby will be fascinated by the texture before they inevitably try to put it into their mouths.

Sight

To develop your infant's sight, invest in brightly coloured toys. The colour will attract them and keep their playtime exciting. When their hands and eyes work together your baby responds quickly to different stimuli. You can expect to see good hand-eye coordination and organized purposeful movements.

Smells

You can save jars of scented products and see which one they love most. For example, let them inhale the scent of vanilla, strawberry, orange or lavender. They will react to the smells and you may notice they prefer one over the other. A familiar scent can help them calm down or stimulate their appetite. Babies love sweet smells that excite them but make sure the scents are from natural products.

Taste

Since babies are drawn to brightly coloured items, place colourful food on their plate and let your baby pick them up one by one. For example, you can place pieces of strawberry, cucumber, tomato and peach on a plate. This allows the baby to improve their eye-hand-mouth coordination while seeing different colours and indulging their taste buds.

Common Challenges With 9 To 12-Month-Old Babies

Teething Tantrums

Your baby is still sprouting new teeth. This can be uncomfortable and painful. You can expect a few tantrums when the discomfort becomes too much for the infant. When your baby is experiencing discomfort give them a cool moist washcloth to chew on and try to distract them. Take them for a walk outdoors, try giving them cuddles, or give them a toy. Sometimes you may need to visit the doctor to get them a prescription for pain relief. Alternatively you can use over the counter medicines such as Baby Paracetamol (Calpol) or baby Ibuprofen. Ensure correct dosage is always followed.

Safety

The baby has learned more about safety because of the smart measures you have taken. As your baby grows it is important to teach them about things that are potentially hazardous. For example, you can point to a knife or an empty bottle of bleach and say "no".

Do not leave these or other dangerous items lying around just because you think you have taught your infant not to touch them. Always keep dangerous items out of reach. Lock your drawers and lower cabinets to prevent your baby from accessing the items within. Lock up any household cleaning products and medicines in areas that are completely out of reach, such as in a locked closet or garage.

Here are some baby dangers in the home:

- Hot beverages like coffee/tea
- Lower drawers and cabinets without a child lock
- Furniture with pointed edges like a desk, table, or even the cot
- Fireplace
- Stairs
- Electrical sockets
- Power cables for electronic appliances like lamps and phone charger
- Electronic appliances like a curling iron, toaster or computer
- Household cleaning products
- Exotic pets like spiders or reptiles
- Windows
- Balconies
- Cosmetics and perfumes

Do not ever leave your toddler alone in the car even if they are sleeping and you will only be gone a minute. When in the home, sleeping children should be checked upon regularly to ensure they are comfortable and safe.

Feeding Issues

Some children are picky eaters. They may reject something that they ate with enthusiasm only last week. Always have a versatile approach to food when it comes to your infant. If they refuse one food emphatically, try something else with the aim of reintroducing the rejected food some other time. Resist the urge to use a stern voice with the baby when they reject food. Kindness and empathy is more likely to get them to eat the food. Do not feed sweets and candy. If you want to give something sweet, choose natural sweets like fruit.

Common Questions About 9 To 12-Month-Old Babies

Can a 9-month-old walk?

Most nine-month-olds do not walk yet, but some do. Babies develop at slightly different rates, and most will be walking soon. Do not be surprised to see your baby crawl up the stairs if you haven't baby proofed your house. These are signs that they will be on their feet soon and running around. It is okay to let your baby crawl on the staircase as long as you are there to supervise and support them.

How can I encourage the cognitive development of my 12-month-old?

There are things you can do like asking simple questions. For example, "Where is your toy?" Hide their toys and look for them together. Lead them right to where the toys are and let them find them. Act surprised and praise them for finding them. Next, hide the toys while they are watching and see if they can find them when you ask where they are.

Can I continue to breastfeed my 9-12-month-old?

It is okay to breastfeed your nine-12-month-old baby as part of their regular diet. Paediatricians recommend that after the first four to six months of exclusively breastfeeding the baby, you should continue regular breastfeeding in addition to feeding other food. The WHO (World Health Organisation) recommends that babies should be breastfed for at least two years.

Breastfeeding should be done after they have eaten their daily solid foods, before a nap or in the morning. This routine ensures that the baby is still able to eat their solid meals first.

Chapter Seven: One to Two Years Old

"I love these little people; and it is not a slight thing when they, who are so fresh from God, love us." – Charles Dickens

Developmental Expectations

At this age the baby is now a toddler and has shown tremendous growth in their cognitive, language, motor and emotional skills. Your child is now able to:

- Walk with less assistance
- Feed themselves independently
- Kick or throw a ball
- Walk backwards and sideways
- Pull or push their toys
- Take things apart
- Take off their shoes
- Speak some words
- Follow simple instructions

For the past year your baby has been growing non-stop. During this coming year the growth spurt they have been experiencing will plateau. Between the age of one and two years your baby will grow by 7.6-12.7 cm in height and 1.5-2.5 kg in weight.

The baby is now able to paint and scribble on paper. They are also growing in their problem-solving abilities so invest in toys that will help them with this skill. For example, puzzles or shape matching toys.

Breastfeeding A Toddler

Toddlers can continue breastfeeding at this age but mums will provide less feedings as the baby eats more solid food. The baby still enjoys the closeness with mum during breastfeeding. Don't worry if their breastfeeding is erratic. Soon they may not even want to nurse at all. Weaning your baby is easiest when it comes naturally so as soon as you notice your baby is nursing less and less, you can stop offering it to them as often and then stop nursing them altogether.

From The Nappy To The Potty

After the first year you may notice fewer nappies are being used and wonder if it is time to start potty training. If you are asking yourself this question then look for some of these tell-tale signs that the baby is ready to learn to use the potty.

- Your toddler stays dry during nap time.
- They have regular bowel movements.
- They are vocal about having a wee or a poo.
- They don't like dirty nappies and will notice when they have wet their nappy.

All children are a bit different as to when they hit their potty milestone. It may take some time to learn to use the potty. While potty training, your little one still needs a nappy to ensure a smooth transition.

To begin the process, play up the positives of using a potty to the child. When you change their nappy, tell them, "Soon you will be using the potty like mummy," or "Soon you won't need a nappy." Build up the excitement and anticipation before you introduce the potty.

When talking to them about going to the bathroom use real words like "Do you want to urinate?" Experts recommend using such language to prevent your child getting used to slang words that will embarrass them in the future. Make the process of going to the bathroom natural by inviting your toddler to sit on their potty when you use the loo if you are comfortable doing this.

Dress your baby for potty success. Pull down clothes or lift up dresses should be the main clothes during this period until they get used to the motion of undressing for potty. Give them practice by encouraging them to pull down or lift their own clothes during a nappy change.

Show your toddler how to squat, sit, wipe and flush. Also, make sure you have the right potty for your toddler. Look for a model that is strong and sturdy to prevent it from tipping over when your little one is using it. If your toddler doesn't want to use the potty and prefers the grown up toilet, you can buy a potty seat for them. It attaches onto the toilet seat, however, you must make sure it is secure. A shaky seat may scare your toddler right back into nappies, or worse they could fall. You will also need a step so they can get up.

How To Develop Their Emotional Intelligence

As their cognitive skills develop you have the incredible role of encouraging healthy emotional intelligence (EQ). This is their ability to express and manage their feelings appropriately. Experts point out that a child with a high EQ is likely to have a high IQ as well. Here are a few tips to help them develop their EQ:

Label Their Feelings

To help them along this journey you can teach your child to label their emotions. If something upsets them ask gently, "Are you angry?" or "Are you sad?" When they are happy ask them, "Are you happy?" These words will become part of their vocabulary and allow them to express their feelings.

Empathize

When your little one is unhappy or sad, show them empathy. Toddlers can be adorably dramatic in their anger. No matter how they manifest their emotions do not trivialize their feelings or chastise them. For example, don't say, "You shouldn't be crying over a biscuit." If your toddler is upset because they can't have another biscuit, say something like, "I also feel upset when I can't eat lots of biscuits, but I must stop so I don't get a tummy ache and can't play. You don't want that, do you?" Once your toddler sees that you understand their feelings, they are more likely to settle down.

Show Them Better Ways To Express Themselves

Your toddler needs to learn how to express their feelings appropriately. Throwing tantrums, screaming and throwing items is not okay. Let them know how you feel when they do something naughty and ask them why they are upset. Acknowledge their feelings and find a solution if you can. Try to encourage them to be able to approach you, and communicate how they feel, affirming you are there to help them.

Teach Them To Self-calm

Teach your little one coping skills that will help them to calm themselves down when they are upset. Let them know that before talking to someone when they are upset they should take a few deep breaths to calm down. Show them how to breathe deeply to calm yourself down. This technique can also be used when coping with fear. Also, invest in a colouring book that your child can use as a calming tool.

Sleep Training Your 1 To 2-Year-Old Toddler

Sleep training techniques work on children 12-months-old and older. Babies younger than this still need their parents to help them fall asleep. Use the following techniques to teach your toddler to fall asleep on their own.

Check And Console Technique

Check in on the baby at pre-set intervals to make sure that they are sleeping. If they are not, do not pick them up or feed them to lull them to sleep. Let them play in their cot and tire themselves out. If they see you and cry out for you, go in and give them a cuddle, rock them a little bit and lay them down again.

Chair Method

Feed your baby and put them down to sleep but don't leave the room. Sit on a chair close enough for them to see you. If they wake up let them see you seated. When they fall asleep you can leave the room. If they wake up crying, pick them up, soothe them and lay them back to sleep while drowsy and sit where they can see you. With time you can move the chair further and further away.

Pick Up, Pat And Shush

Your baby is used to your touch so don't deprive them of it. This method emphasizes holding the baby until they stop crying, you can provide a small bounce as you hold them, or pat them on the back to provide comfort. Then lie them down to sleep, and try shushing them with a soft voice. Give it a few minutes, and if they continue to cry then pick them up, soothe them again, and put them down as they become drowsy and let them fall asleep.

Bedtime Routine

This is the most important strategy of all! This technique involves putting the baby down to sleep at the same time every day. As your little one grows they get into the routine you have set for them, and they are likely tired by the same time each evening. Your baby may fuss for a few minutes when you lie them down, however they will eventually be too tired to fight off the sleep.

Common Questions About 1 To 2-Year-Old Toddlers

Will it be harder to wean my baby if I breastfeed them longer than a year?

This question may stem from a common warning given to new mums that if you don't wean your baby early, you will not be able to do it. This is not true. Breastfeeding past your baby's first birthday doesn't make it harder to get them off the breast. Your little one has their own developmental timeline which prepares them for weaning. Some babies will stop breastfeeding before the first year is over (but this is highly unusual) while others will stop by their second or third birthday. Let weaning happen naturally.

Can I still nurse my toddler if I now have another baby?

Yes you can! This is called tandem nursing and it is completely safe as long as you follow certain guidelines. To begin with, nurse the infant first and more often. This is because after your baby is born, your milk contains colostrum which is essential for the new-born's health. After your new-born is satisfied you can now nurse your toddler.

Talking to your toddler is important to help them understand that their little brother or sister needs to feed first. Your toddler may not even like the taste of the new milk so they may not want to nurse as much. However, when the mature milk comes in they may resume enthusiastic nursing. They may not like it at first, but with time your toddler will understand and patiently wait their turn.

The good news, at least for your tots, is that the more they breastfeed the more milk mum produces. In a few weeks the mother's breasts will have enough supply to feed both little ones. This is the same as someone who is nursing twins. Mums should be prepared for breast milk to leak because of the overabundant milk supply.

If tandem nursing, make sure you consult your doctor to ensure that your new-born is monitored by observing their growth, and that they are receiving enough nutrients. If tandem nursing is your choice don't feel pressured to wean the older child unless your doctor advises it.

Chapter Eight: Three Years Old

"Children must be taught how to think, not what to think." - Margaret Mead

It has been two full years since you brought your bundle of joy home and now they can toddle around and are getting into things. Their motor skills have grown exponentially and they are speaking a bit. Going into their third year, you probably still have lots of questions.

At this age, they require more room to get out all that energy. Do you have a tricycle yet? They're probably ready to pedal. Go ahead and put them on one and supervise them as they ride down the sidewalk or path. Also, don't be surprised to see them trying to outrun you when you are playing outdoors.

Your baby is also able to cut and snip with scissors and draw lines and circles. This is because their coordination has grown immensely. A toddler at this age can brush their teeth and dress or undress with a little help. Independent kids will want to do this without any assistance. It is okay to let them and rectify any "mishaps" later.

They can use the potty with fewer accidents and more confidence. They are also able to handle basic hygiene like washing their hands after using the potty. Allow them to use a fork and spoon during feeding times but expect a mess.

Their cognitive development (mental capacity) has grown and this is making them better problem solvers. There is less frustration or crying when things don't work the way they want. Instead you will notice more concentration and thinking involved in their play.

Better Understanding of the Language

In the third year your toddler has over 200 words in their vocabulary. They are able to absorb more words from you as you speak. Keep reading to them since they will learn new words this way.

Get more verbally interactive with your child. For example, you can ask your child what they want to do with their day. Get their opinion on what you should do together. This helps them learn that their thoughts and opinions matter in the family.

Common Challenges Faced with 3 Year Olds

Tantrums

Your toddler is experiencing a lot of emotion when they throw a tantrum. Seeing it this way helps you better understand why they are behaving in that manner. If you are in a public place, try to take your toddler to a secluded spot and ask them why they are upset. Then you can calm them down and explain the situation. If they do not calm down you may need to sit with them until they do. However, do not take them home on account of the tantrum because this will set a pattern you want to avoid. Remember, if there is something that they need, and you are not providing it, such as food, sleep or clean nappies, it is understandable that they are upset.

Defiance

Your little one is growing into their personality and unfortunately this comes with a phase of defiance. They may ignore you when you give them instructions like "pick up your toys" or "stop banging your toy." It is normal for toddlers to test your limits.

If they ignore your instruction the first time, issue the instruction a second time in case they didn't hear you. If you know they heard you, also include a warning this time. If the defiance continues follow through with the warning. For example: "Stop banging your toys or I will take them all away." If the banging persists, take the toys away for a period of time to show them the consequence of their actions.

Feeding Problems

You may have a picky eater or a toddler who claims to be hungry within a short period of time after the last meal. Help your little one to have a healthy relationship with food by not force feeding picky eaters and not over indulging those with big appetites. Praise all types of food using words like "delicious" and "yummy". This is a vocabulary that your toddler will understand as opposed to words like "healthy".

Consider the role of food and scheduling before you declare a feeding issue a problem. For example, did they have a sweet snack in the late afternoon? If dinner is early, they might not be hungry yet. Similarly, if you are not providing meals on a consistent schedule, your child may overfeed when they get access to food.

Disrespectful Behaviour

Spitting, biting, mocking you or name calling must be addressed immediately. If not addressed, this behaviour will only grow worse with time. Some parents prefer to ignore certain behaviours so the toddler sees that their bad behaviour doesn't get them attention.

However, firmer discipline may work more effectively as it shows that the consequence for such behaviour is severe. For example, if your tot takes to name calling, remove their favourite toy or put them on time out for a while. This clearly shows them the offensive nature of their behaviour. In the future, they will likely be afraid of the same consequences for misbehaving.

Whining is another bad behaviour that kids can get used to using to get attention. If you give in to the whining, they will learn that this behaviour will help them get their way. Curb this behaviour before it becomes a habit.

Impulsive Behaviour

Young children are impulsive by nature and some can act out. You need to curtail your little one's impulsive behaviours by encouraging them to verbalize their feelings instead of acting out physically. This is why it is important to teach your toddler to manage their feelings as explained in the previous chapter. Emotional intelligence will help them cope better in upsetting situations.

Preparing Your Toddler for Nursery/Social Interaction

Nursery school will be a new concept for your baby because it is likely that they have not been around a lot of other children yet. It is also likely that you have not been apart very much. To prepare, you can play pretend preschool with your little one or take them to places where they will have more social interactions with other toddlers.

Consider taking them to the preschool so they can have a tour and see other kids at play. This will give them a real picture of this new environment and build anticipation about the new experience. They can even talk to a teacher. Practice getting ready and going to the location and inside the building if they will let you. Don't make a big deal about it, or you will make both of you anxious. If any anxiety comes up about attending pre-school, listen to their worries and talk through each of them.

How to Nurture Independence in Your Toddler

You are likely to get a very enthusiastic response from your toddler when you begin to teach them independence. They are raring to go! Get their independence going by asking them to do things by themselves. For example, tell them, "It's time to put on your t-shirt. Can you do it by yourself?" They are happy to prove to you that they can. Praise them when they do something correctly on their own. If they do it incorrectly, gently help them correct it.

It is important to identify opportunities to foster independence in your toddler. Hand washing, hair brushing, brushing their teeth and putting away their toys are some of the small tasks you can give them. This will teach them independence and responsibility. Also, teach them to place their dirty clothes in the laundry basket. Praise every little effort.

Common Questions About 3 Year Olds

Can you reason with a 3 year old?

At this point, your little one is able to ask "why", and understand the logic of asking a question and getting an answer. They are very curious and this is how they gather information. This is why they ask you questions like, "Why does this work that way?" or "Why is that done this way?" They will ask why about almost everything they can and in the process they learn many things. Don't expect them to remember all the answers, and expect them to ask you the same questions more than once as they learn. Because of their association with the word "why", it is helpful to reason with them by using the word "why" followed by an explanation.

For example, if your toddler is playing too rough with other children you can pose a question to them after making a statement about their behaviour:

Statement and Question: "You are playing too rough. Do you know why it is bad to play rough?"

Explanation: "It's because you can hurt your friend and you don't want that do you? If you hurt them they probably won't want to play with you again. That is why it is bad to play rough with your friend. Do you understand?"

How do I discipline my toddler?

Set limits and stay consistent with discipline, but be flexible according to the situation. Learn not to overreact to your child's behaviour when they are frustrated or don't want to obey. Children learn by example so being a calm parent will foster a calm demeanour in your little one.

Understanding a child is essential in administering discipline. The discipline style you settle on is more dependent on the personality of the child and how they respond to various discipline styles. A super sensitive child has very different needs from those of an exuberant one. Single parents have to shoulder the entire responsibility of disciplining their little one so make sure that any adult who helps you care for your child maintains the same type of discipline.

For most children at this age, emphatic redirection is adequate. This means telling them no in an angry voice, stopping their actions, explaining why and redirecting them to something else that is positive. For example, if they throw their toy, you say, "No, we don't throw our toys because you might break your toy." Go get the toy and bring it back and show them the correct way to play with it, telling them. "See, this is how we play nice with our toys." Praise them when they do it correctly.

Remember, at this age, children are rarely behaving badly on purpose. Many are just exploring new behaviours and trying to express themselves. It is important that you teach them right from wrong, and that you do it in a way that is positive to their growth and your relationship with them.

Also remember that you have a responsibility to ensure that there is nothing specific causing the behaviour that is out of their control. If the child is frustrated because of a situation beyond their control, you need to address the situation first and then determine if there is a need for discipline for the child's actions. For example, are you at the park? Are they crying and yelling and trying to get away? Maybe they got bit by a wasp. If they are hungry, tired or have to go to the bathroom, they might throw a bit of a tantrum, because they are upset and are trying to express themselves. It is up to you to rectify these things and get your child back to a happy place. A happy child is a happy parent!

Final Words

Parenting is one of the greatest adventures you can have in life. Whether you are doing it alone, or with a strong support network, raising a child will have highs and lows. You can reduce the anxiety of not knowing what to do by practicing the fundamentals explored in this book.

Babies are so fragile as they start life and you may be nervous about doing everything right. Don't worry, if you have prepared mentally and physically, and have acquired all the important basics, you are off on the right foot! From there, simply follow the age specific guidelines in this book to remind yourself of what to expect as they grow.

Soon enough you will start to see them coming into their own. They will be less dependent on you as time goes by, and will be exploring the world around them.

This book has highlighted the milestones to expect as your baby grows into a toddler. These milestones are not cast in stone. Every child is different and unique. Embrace the individuality of your special little human as they grow, and embrace your new role as the most important figure in their life.

These first few years are precious and ever changing. May you and your baby enjoy the journey of life together and make it as wonderful as it can be.

Printed in Great Britain
by Amazon